The Grace Of My Lover (Jesus)

Written by: Marilyn Lacy

This book is dedicated to my parents whom I love and miss dearly, Leonard Lacy & Marilyn Lewis, and my beautiful children. I love y'all more than all the stars, in all the sky, in all the world. I am absolutely convinced my life was spared because of the purpose and destiny God has for each of you. I'm thankful to God for His grace and His mercy. He snatched me out of darkness, even when I was willing to stay there, and led me into the light of His absolute truth. He has given me a heart to forgive others and myself. He has given me a heart to serve.

I'm grateful to God for all of the people who will be set free by His loving grace and the blood from His son Jesus Christ. The love of our Lord and Savior surpasses all understanding. He truly has a reckless love for us. When we make the decision to accept Him as our Lord and Savior, and choose to seek first the kingdom of God and all of His righteousness, He promises to meet our every need.

And Hannah prayed and said: "My heart rejoices in the Lord; My horn is exalted in the Lord. I smile at my enemies, Because I rejoice in Your salvation"

"No one is holy like the Lord, For there is none besides You, Nor is there any rock like our God."

1 Samuel 2:1-2 NKJV

Table of Contents:

Introduction 1

My Early Days and Family Relations 2

Living with Dysfunction 8

My Sister's Father and the Start of My Feelings of Hopelessness 12

Drugs, Relationships, Other Habits and Addictions 17

The Start of the Journey from Darkness to Light 33

Breaking the Concrete Around My Heart 46

What the Redeemer Has Given Me: Purpose 71

INTRODUCTION

I thank God for where I am today. He has kept His hand over my life, and He did not let me perish when He could have so many times. He knew the plan He had for my life (*Jeremiah 29:11*). I wrote this book with the hope of inspiring and encouraging others to seek for themselves a personal relationship with God, to give glory and honor to God for what He has done and still is doing in my life through His son Jesus Christ and the Holy Spirit. Because of my surrender to His will, my commitment to do my best to live a life that's pleasing to Him and have a heart after His own.

And I, if I am lifted up from the earth, will draw all peoples to Myself. John 12:32 NKJV

And I will do this when I am lifted up off the ground and when I draw the hearts of people to gather them to me. John 12:32 TPT

Trust in the Lord with all your heart, And lean not on your own understanding Proverbs 3:4 NKJV

Then you will find favor and high regard with God and people. Proverbs 3:4 CSB

My Early Days and Family Relations

By the time most of my childhood memories that could be easily recalled were taking place, my mom and dad were not together anymore; she was married to my brother's dad, who I came to love as my dad. My parents had never married, and I don't ever remember them together as a couple. They had broken up when I was about one and a half, according to my mom.

We lived with my brother's dad for a few years, and it was cool. He spent as much time as he could with me. We never had a lot of material things, but I had everything I needed. When the seasons would change, my long pants became cut-off shorts. I remember the fringes on my homemade jean shorts that my step dad decided to burn off. What stands out in my mind is FIRE!!!

He set the whole rim of my shorts on fire. It happened so fast, but he put it out before I could get burned. I was terrified at the time, but looking back, it's one of the funniest memories I have from childhood.

I remember one day while riding my bike, I was stung by a bee. My stepdad put ice on the sting, and it hurt so much, more than anything I'd ever felt before. My stepdad was a good dad, he was very good to me. Though it didn't work out with him and my mom. They divorced. I'm not sure who came into our lives after him, there were different guys over time, My mom wanted us to have a "dad."

I grew up with lots of family around. Both of my grandmothers were really big influences in my life, both sweet, loving and funny homemakers. Very loving. They had amazing hearts, and I never doubted their love for me. I had a very special bond with each of them. I only knew one of my grandfathers, my dad's father. We had a pretty good relationship even though we didn't really talk much. I don't recall any bad experiences with him. It always seemed like there was an elephant in the room that we tried hard to ignore. I always wanted to ask him about the relationship between him and grandma...I just didn't have the guts. My mom's father died before I was born. I heard both my grandfathers were very abusive to my grandmothers. Both grandfathers struggled with alcoholism and both probably endured physical and or verbal abuse when they were children. I was told, one day while drunk, my mom's dad beat my grandma and had it not been for my uncle, would have shot her with a shotgun. Through the abuse, they both stayed. He died years later from complications due to years of alcohol abuse. Staying is just what you did back then, now that I think about it, some people are 'still staying' today.

My grandfather (my dad's father) after years of marriage, left my grandmother for her niece, whom he stayed in relationship with until he died. My grandmother was giving all honor at his military funeral since they had never divorced. Despite all they endured, my grandmothers were very strong, honorable women, and I loved them very much. I still do.

My mom's mother could have easily been employed as a comedian. She was always talking about hitting somebody with her lug nut remover she kept under her bed. She kept us laughing. She gave me two nicknames: Red Bird, and Pippy Long Stockings. I spent a lot of time at her house because she kept my siblings and I while my mom worked. She'd given birth to ten children; nine survived, and one she delivered was deceased. They all have the comedic bone, all of us do. They passed it down to us. I always thought we'd all live together one day, we'd stay that way forever.

My dad's mom gave birth to six children. Four boys, two girls. Both of my grandmothers raised their children the very best they could and considering the circumstances, they did extremely well.

I take my hat off to them, I admire their strength. I miss them so much. Not a day goes by that I don't reminisce and think about them and the time I spent watching them cook, learning how to sew, getting wisdom poured into me... even though I didn't know it at the time. Seeds of knowledge were being planted. I wish I had been mature enough to sit longer at their feet, not rush off, spend as much time as I could soaking it all up. What I wouldn't give for more time with them.

As a young girl, I spent a lot of time playing with my cousins. We'd spend our days running through the neighborhood, linking up with our friends from school, not a care in the world. Just having fun. My cousins and I were together all the time, we all lived in the same housing projects, and sometimes the same house. These were wonderful times, the best times. All of us together. We laughed so much. Sometimes there was arguing and fighting, It was how we communicated. How we'd learned to communicate. Even with the arguing, it was all love. The only way we knew how to love. When all you know is all you know, that's what you do, we learn what we see. Don't think I'd trade those times for anything, I wouldn't..

And now abide faith, hope, love, these three; but the greatest of these is love. 1 Corinthians 13:13 NKJV

My dad and I didn't spend a lot of time together when I was younger, or as a young adult because of his heroin addiction. He broke a lot of promises but it didn't stop me from believing the next promise he made. I believe his intentions were good, in fact, I know his intentions were good. There's no doubt in my mind the hurt he caused me...he didn't intentionally hurt me, he was bound by strongholds and demons he couldn't free himself from. He lived through childhood trauma (s) and never healed or surrendered those things to God. I don't know if he even knew how to. I hear people talk about generational curses, the more I learn I think it would be better labeled generational choices. Some of us are repeating choices made in our families that have not been positive or fruitful. Things were a lot different when he was young. Silence. Suffer in silence. Don't talk about such things. Don't tell your family business (still alive in some homes today) We learn what we see. When I got older, when I could, I'd spend nights at my grandma's house so I could spend time with him; which wasn't as often as I would've liked because my mother knew what he was doing. Spending time together meant him taking me along to buy heroin or riding around town giving people rides so he could get money to buy heroin. I'd hang out with him, his girlfriend or his buddies. Hanging out meaning I'd be watching them nod and go in and out of consciousness. At the time it didn't matter to me (I didn't think it did) I just wanted to be with him. I loved being with him, he was my dad, I didn't see him negatively. I didn't judge him, no matter what anyone said about him, no matter how many empty or broken promises he made, I looked forward to going to see him and had some of the best times with him, adventures... in my mind. There were times we picked up women and gave them rides that turned into hilarious situations, going into stores shoplifting and running from security, walking through the grocery store eating food off the shelf without paying for it, Not your typical visit with dad I know, still, that's what it was when I was with him and I very much longed to spend time with him and have a relationship with my father. Like God longs for a relationship with us. He is our heavenly Father, He loves us so much and He wants to save us from our sins so we can spend eternity with Him, and also have a relationship with Him while we're here on earth so He can help us navigate through life.

"For God so loved the world that He gave His only begotten Son, that whosoever believes in Him should not perish but have everlasting life." John 3:16 NKJV

The fact is, my mom had also survived childhood trauma (s) that she never talked about, and because of it spent years in and out of abusive relationships. Every relationship I can recall her being in was abusive with the exception of one or two, and one of those men was married so that relationship didn't last long. When it came down to choice, he chose his wife and children. To experience verbal, emotional, physical, and mental abuse were almost daily occurrences in my house even though I didn't know those "labels" at the time. Most men my mom dated didn't respect her, my brother, sister or myself. I never understood (until now) why she lacked self-worth, or why she tolerated abuse, why she felt she deserved it, or didn't deserve better. When growing up, the environment we live in shapes us into who we become as adults. It's not often realized that we will eventually repeat behaviors or allow certain behaviors because we've learned that it's ok. It's love. Our parents, or whoever has raised us are our first teachers, for some, the only teachers. We must be very intentional not to repeat learned unhealthy behavior. It's important we look to our Heavenly Father to teach us the correct way, His way, to love, nurture, correct, discipline etc...it's why our salvation and relationship with God matters most. When we ask Abba, He gives.

"Most assuredly, I say to you, whatever you ask the Father in My name He will give you." John 16:23 NKJV

In that day you will not ask me anything. Truly I tell you, anything you ask the Father in my name, he will give you. John 16:23 CSB

Living with Dysfunction

As time passed, for whatever reason we had to move in with my aunt. At the time, her house, back then, was the party house (more like a brothel). She and her friends would go to the bar, spend the day there until it closed, and back to my aunt's house everyone would come. The house was small, three bedrooms, one bathroom, in the projects. By the time we'd moved in with her, there were nine of us in that three bedroom house: my aunt, her boyfriend, her four children; my mom, myself, and my brother...not to mention the people who stayed over when they were too drunk to go home. It was not a good environment to grow up in. I say that now, but then, I didn't know it. There was always a lot of action, excitement and fun. When you're a child you don't know any better. To me they were fun times, looking back and knowing what I know now, it was very dysfunctional. There was dysfunction passed down from generation to generation. I learned to live with it. There was a lot of love wrapped up in that dysfunction. Honestly, until I was much older and introduced to different environments, met different people and active in counseling, I had no idea I grew up in a "dysfunctional" household. The way I saw it was...at least I ate everyday, even if sometimes it was only mayonnaise or tomato sandwiches, I had food in my stomach. I never went hungry. We had a roof over our heads, her house was always clean and when my aunt did cook, which was more often than not, she would throw-down in the kitchen. My aunt, next to my grandma, was the best cook. We were not necessarily a praying family but I heard about God, I knew who He was. I knew I was supposed to look to Him for help when I needed it. I'd hear stories from my grandma (maternal) about how she had prayed to God for whatever help she needed, how she'd carried her burdens to Him because they were too heavy for her. If she was ailing, she'd pray for relief. All this outside of church, which I only remember her attending a few times on an Easter Sunday, she was what's known as a "bedside baptist." I witnessed her relationship with Him. She had quite the cussin' spirit that would rise up in her when she got irritated, then bless you real good when she was happy. I felt the tugging of God early, there was a feeling I couldn't explain, a pulling inside me. I wasn't really interested in a lot of things other kids my age were doing, I was a loner. I only participated with the other kids so I wouldn't be made fun of and I was still made fun of. I always felt like an outcast with my peers. I believe God wanted to draw me closer to Him when I was younger, but because of events that would take place, I would spend most of my life running from Him and destroying myself in the process.

"Have I not commanded you? Be strong and of good courage; do not be afraid or dismayed for the LORD your God is with you wherever you go." Joshua 1:9 NKJV

I met my best friend in the 1st grade, and we've been like sisters ever since. We were always together when we were younger, nothing could separate us. We've gone through a lot together. We spent our teen years wild and out of control. Doing any and just about anything (and anyone) sad to say, we were so misguided and looking for love in all the wrong places. Outside of Christ, we can't know what true love is. We've had a few differences over the years, but our sisterhood truly has stood the test of time. You wanna hear it? Here it is...at the time, before the revision of this book, I truly believed in my heart we were best friends. I mean, how could we not be? We met in first grade and spent most of all our teen years inseparable. You rarely saw one of us without the other, so much so, even people who knew us growing up called us by each other's names. I guess there were things I chose to overlook over the years regarding our relationship, for the sake of our friendship and what it meant to me. Her chasing after my boyfriend (s) was something I thought was "teenage stuff" and I didn't really pay any attention to. In all honesty, it wasn't until I began to go through my most difficult times in adulthood that I realized well, I'll just say things (our friendship) were put into perspective. It's ok to grow up. It's ok to grow apart. It happens. There's no love lost.

I didn't realize I had begun to feel resentment toward my father because I didn't see him much, he spent his time high or trying to get high. I felt he loved heroin more than me. I felt it took priority over his relationship with me. I always felt I had to compete with his addiction and I had no way of knowing how to do that. I wanted to feel important, like I mattered to him. I wanted and needed to know he saw me. I would share stories with him and halfway through he'd look unconscious. I had no idea how his absence was influencing my world. He was the most important man in my life and I felt invisible to him. I was angry that I had to live with my mom and her boyfriend (s) who didn't even like me. I didn't come to that conclusion until I was older (I resented him) even though my dad and I didn't have a traditional father-daughter relationship, I longed for his presence, and his attention. It's just a natural thing, wanting and needing affection from your father. I've learned it is one of the most important relationships, the relationship of a young girl and her father. It will play a huge role in the man / men she will choose to be in a relationship with later in life. My dad never turned into an adult in my eyes, he never had his own place with any responsibility, he either lived with my grandfather or grandmother so I always knew where to find him. When he wasn't out copping, he was in the house. No matter how high, he would always find me on my birthday each year, if nothing else was consistent seeing him on my birthday was...he'd say "Happy Birthday, how old are you again?" I felt sad, and happy he had remembered my birthday. The older I got, I started to feel like I didn't have a father. I would hear other girls my age talk about their relationship with their dad and I'd be envious. What was it about me that my dad didn't want to be a part of my life? I didn't understand. Believe me, it consumed me trying to figure it out. Nothing compares to the feeling of unwantedness by someone who assisted in giving you life. It's heartbreaking.

"Be of good courage, And He shall strengthen your heart, And you who hope in the Lord." Psalm 31:24 NKJV

Be strong and let your heart be courageous, all you who put your hope in the LORD. Psalm 31:24 CSB

So cheer up! Take courage, all who love him. Wait for him to break through for you, all who trust in him. Psalm 31:24 TPT

"Do not sorrow, for the joy of the Lord is your strength" Nehemiah 8:10 NKJV

My Sister's Father and the Start of My Feelings of Hopelessness

I was eight years old when my mom met my sister's father. I'm not sure how long they were dating before she felt comfortable enough to introduce him to my brother and I, which we never formally were. We were still living with my aunt and he came to spend the night one night. After hours of card playing and drinking he came into the room while my mom was still downstairs. He laid beside me on the floor mattress and started rubbing on me and tried to unzip my pants. I jumped up and told my older cousin who was also sleeping in the room what he'd done. She got up, turned the lights on "what are you doing" she asked. He told her my pants were open and he was trying to button them. Lie!! "He's lying, I'm telling my mom!" I said.

I went to find my mom to tell her what he'd done. He repeated the same lie he'd told to my cousin, my pants were open and I was trying to button them. My mom became very angry with me, "Why were your pants open!!?" she yelled. "Go lay down!" she said angrily. He had a smirk on his face like...Oh yeah, I got her. He knew at that moment he could tell my mom anything and she'd believe him, she'd believe him over me. She didn't give it a second thought. She never asked me what happened, asked me to explain, nothing. It was as if I was at fault and she didn't want to talk about it.

I was hurt and confused, I didn't understand why she yelled at me. I thought she would be on my side. I knew for sure she wouldn't see him anymore but he became a more permanent part of my life seeing as my mom had fallen head over heels for him. He was, in her own words, the love of her life.

Some time passed and we moved from my aunt's house and into his mom's house. Shortly after we moved in, she (his mom) and her husband moved to Arizona and left the house to him and my mom. I was so happy to live in that house, it was so big, bigger than any place we'd lived before. I loved living there, until... I didn't. The saying goes... it's all good til it aint.

I spent the next several years of my childhood being molested and forced to do unspeakable things with and to him every time my mother left the house. He would force me to do things that I knew he shouldn't be doing with me. He always did things that he knew couldn't be proven. He never penetrated me, he performed oral and other perverted acts on me and forced me to do the same to him. It took me years to build up the courage to tell my 6th grade Science teacher what was happening to me at home. That felt like the best day of my life, the reality would be it turned out to be the worst day of my life. I was finally free from keeping that shameful secret, I thought...finally it's over, but I didn't get any support from my mom. My mother was so angry I went to school and told a "lie" as she called it, our mother- daughter relationship ended that day. From that day on, she treated me like she hated me. Not one day, not a single day went by that I didn't regret telling. The dynamic changed so drastically. There was a sour taste in my mom's mouth for me and I knew it. It was evident and obvious to others as well. She spoke negatively to me and about me to everyone she'd talk to. Telling them how grown I was. Throwing myself at him and he'd refused my advances so I made up a story, made up a "sick story". She would constantly tell me I was sick and I needed help. Our living situation changed when I exposed the abuse and we had to move back in with my aunt. Telling what he did to me destroyed everything. He cried like a baby, saying he didn't know why I would lie on him, "I love her like she's my own child" he said. I remember my mom consoling him telling him not to worry, she believed him and knew he wouldn't do anything like that to me. Some part of me died inside when he started abusing me, but to have my mom not believe me and side with him...It was a double homicide. I lost touch with myself. I didn't feel anymore. I disconnected from myself. Another person was born in me that day to cope with it all. My brother and sister were still very young, and because I told my teacher, the school called the police. There was an investigation, and I was told by my mother that if I didn't tell them I was lying about what he'd done to me, my brother, sister, and myself would be taken away. We'd be separated and wouldn't see each other anymore. The strain, the hurt, the thought of my brother and sister being sent away was too much for me to imagine.

In my interview with the detectives, I told them I'd made the story up because I was angry about being punished. The woman detective who interviewed me begged me to tell the truth, she'd been trained to see the signs, the pain and anguish as I recalled my encounters with him, the relief of releasing it. She asked if someone told me to lie about what happened, with tears running down my face, blurring my vision, all I could think was I would never see my brother and sister again. So I stuck to the lie, that I'd made the whole thing up.

My mom began to tell people, "I told you she was lying, she's crazy" she said. It killed me. I lost my identity and didn't know if I was coming or going. My mom kept asking me why I had lied. Why would I say that about him? "He loves us," she said. "Why did you do this!?" "What have you done!?" When the detectives closed their investigation, my mom was told if she decided to stay with him, my siblings and I would be taken from her. Apparently, he had ex-girlfriends whose daughters said he had done things to them, the same things he'd done to me, so he couldn't live in the house with us anymore. I can't put into words what I felt from my mom, but if I had to, I would say hate. That's what it felt like. With her words, she killed what was left of the little girl inside me. I was almost twelve and a half, I had accepted the words she spoke to me, and tried to make sense of them in my head, but I couldn't. That lie she made me tell killed my hope of ever having a relationship with my mom. I became very bitter, very angry - angry at the world, including myself. I built a concrete wall around myself, around my heart. I vowed no one would ever hurt me again, not without me hurting them back. Every negative emotion I could feel, I felt daily.

When he had to leave, he took with him pieces of me that would take me years to reclaim. He immediately found someone else to play house with, and my mother's resentment toward me was greatly felt. She made my life a living hell. She was so angry with me, the smallest thing would set her off. I was angry too. We would disagree and argue about every issue, there was no communication between us except yelling. My days were filled with hurt, sadness, anguish and despair. I felt hopeless, and would feel that way for years to come. I started having suicidal thoughts. My heart was broken. The pain was absolutely crippling...devastating.

The LORD is near to those who have a broken heart, And saves such as have a contrite spirit. Psalm 34:18 NKJV

The LORD is near the brokenhearted; he saves those crushed in spirit. Psalm 34:18 CSB

The Lord is close to all whose hearts are crushed by pain and he is always ready to restore the repentant one. Psalm 34:18 TPT

Drugs, Relationships, and Other Habits and Addictions

I ran full speed ahead to a road of self-destruction. When I was thirteen, my uncle gave me my first hit of marijuana, and I started drinking. That's when I met my first boyfriend. My mom had moved us from the projects in O'Donnell Heights to Cedonia. Although I was very apprehensive about being in a relationship with a guy, because of the sexual abuse, I wanted to feel loved. Even though I felt like there was a sign on my head that read, "UNCLEAN" or "DAMAGED GOODS." We began dating. I started getting in trouble, fighting in and out of school, anytime, anywhere. I fought all the time, in my mind, my boyfriend was like my knight in shining armor. I eventually told him about the abuse, and he cried with me. I got pregnant with twins at 14, and was forced to have an abortion. I was devastated. Now it was my turn to show hate. I felt like I hated my mom, the sight of her, her voice, everything. In spite of everything that had happened before, up until that point, deep down inside I still very much longed for her love and affection, but not so much after being forced to murder my unborn children. Not at all. I didn't care about her love or affection anymore (that's what my anger and the enemy's voice was telling me) she had a habit of making threats to me, because she was still very bitter over my sister's father, the spankings turned into me being physically beat down. A knock down, dragged, bloody beat down. Now I looked for confrontation from her. I had told myself, "If she ever hits me again, I'm going to hit her back." IF SHE PUT ANOTHER HAND ON ME I'M GOING TO SNAP!!!!! The respect I had for her was totally gone, hers for me...had been gone! I had so much rage built up inside of me; I was a ticking time bomb. I had an eight o'clock curfew, so I'd purposely come in at ten. I was intentionally trying to initiate conflict. She'd hit me because I would argue back and forth with her, frustrating her to the point of physical contact. I spent about a year physically fighting with her. She beat me every time, but that didn't stop me, it's like I wanted to see how much physical pain I could take.

Meanwhile, my relationship with my boyfriend was on the rocks because he'd gotten expelled from our high school for fighting. A girl I went to school with called my house to speak to my mom. She told my mom I was throwing away my birth control pills when I got to school because I was trying to get pregnant again. My mom beat the snot out of me when she got off the phone. Beat! The! Snot! Out! Me! I told my boyfriend the next day in school. I didn't know what he'd do, I always told him everything. When he saw her at school the next day, he beat her almost unconscious and was arrested and expelled. I realized then he was obsessed with me and had serious anger issues. He couldn't see or talk to me because he was on punishment and that enraged him. There was a guy at school who liked me and he'd be waiting in the hall when my class let out. He started walking me to all of my classes, He had been waiting for an opportunity to ask me out, and with my boyfriend out of school, he took advantage of the opportunity. Word got back to my boyfriend that I was dating someone at school. We weren't dating, he was really just walking me to my classes. When I got home from school one day, my boyfriend was sitting in my apartment building. He asked me why I was letting him walk me to class, we began arguing, and he beat me like he beat the girl at school, so bad that the neighbors had to come out their apartment to get him off of me. I didn't see him anymore after that. It was extremely devastating for me, he was my lifeline, my outlet. I looked to him for everything. I had put all my hope into him and our relationship. I really didn't know what to do without him, but I also was conflicted about being with him so I ignored him, his apologies, his letters, his messages through mutual friends, I completely shut him out. My thought was... how can you say you love me and hurt me so badly. I was afraid to imagine what would've been if the neighbor hadn't come out. I was expelled from school almost a year later for fighting. I had a fight with a senior, I was a sophomore, and because of my history of fighting in high school they chose to expel me. I was ordered to go to night school and I did for about a month but I quit. For years, I had experienced so much, when I thought about our relationship, I had only good memories. I didn't know about suppressed memories. I had forgotten the reason why. Why we broke up. Why did we break up? I honestly didn't remember. I thought it was because of everything that had happened, the pregnancy, the running away... our parents forbid us to see each other. Every relationship that followed was abusive, and because of that, the enemy began telling me guys were vile, disgusting, disrespectful beings that couldn't be trusted. I know now that's why we are to put our trust in God. Not man.

You will keep him in perfect peace, Whose mind is stayed on You, Because he trusts in You. Trust in the Lord forever, For in YAH, the Lord, is everlasting strength. Isaiah 26:3-4 NKJV

You will keep the mind that is dependent on you in perfect peace for it is trusting in you. Trust in the LORD forever, because in the LORD, the LORD himself, is an everlasting rock!
Isaiah 26:3-4 CSB

By the time I was about to turn fifteen, my mom was in a relationship with a very violent man. He was good at using and pulling knives on people and during a physical altercation with him he wrapped a telephone cord around my neck and tried to strangle me, we both pulled knives on each other. I couldn't take anymore "dads" so after our last argument and fight, I ran away (again), this time for good. I began living here and there, I couldn't really stay with family because they would tell my mom where I was, except for my aunt we used to live with. I could always stay with her. So that's mainly where I stayed. My mom found out I was staying there and came there with her boyfriend to get me, we had another physical fight and he picked me up and slammed me through my aunt's glass table. I ran outside to my homeboys in the neighborhood, they were going to shoot him, but my conscience couldn't let that happen. I didn't want them to take his life. So, I was fifteen and back in the projects I spent my childhood in. For a short while we lived in Turners Station, another community in Dundalk, but back in O'Donnell Heights I met back up with my girl, my ace. We were living wherever we could, trying to support ourselves. We worked at the Travel Plaza, The Best Western Hotel. It was cool, but we had Champagne taste and Kool - Aid pockets. We wanted money and figured out how to get it. We wanted to look fly. We ran the streets and were approached by a dude her aunt was dating. He had a business proposal for us. He'd supply us with crack cocaine, we'd sell it, and he'd pay us for it. We were hanging on the corners 24/7 anyway, why not? That opened the door to a whole new life. We were exposed to many things. We were getting real money now and soon stopped working at the Travel Plaza. We stayed outside all day, everyday some days. We were like... BALLIN!!!! We couldn't believe the money we were making everyday. No more hustling outside of Joe's Tavern. We used to stand outside of Joe's (the neighborhood bar) asking for money from people going in and out of the bar. We would tell them we'd refused to have sex with some guys and they put us out of the car and we needed to get home. They had no idea we lived up the street. Literally. Even before we started hustling drugs, we were hustling. I was hustling outside the bar before I was old enough to go in, and would end up a barmaid there when I was old enough. When we were almost fifteen we were approached by someone to model lingerie for grown men and women. We caught the eye of a much older man who wanted us to work for him. He wanted us to run a house he had (sit in it and sell crack out of it) When he told us how much he'd pay us, We both realized we were getting played by the other dude that was really only giving us "outfit money." Needless to say, we jumped on the house deal. We sat in a crack house day in and day out, making more money than we'd ever seen. You couldn't tell us we weren't big time. We spent days high off marijuana, and drinking. Two teenagers in a house full of adults who smoked crack all day. The house got raided one day before we got there, we managed to dodge that bullet...so we were back hanging on the corners in our hood. There was an older guy who wanted to date my best friend, he came through the neighborhood one day looking for her. She was with her boyfriend. "Ride to the store with me," he said. I got in the car, we went to the bar and he brought some Cisco. He poured me drink after drink until I was drunk, took me to a motel and raped me. That same guy later beat my father in the face with a table leg because my father took a package (of drugs) from him and didn't pay him back. I wanted to kill him. My father looked unrecognizable, but he left the hospital refusing medical treatment. I always replay the tape of my life and I can clearly see the evidence of God's grace and mercy in my life.

Your mercy, O Lord, is in the heavens; Your faithfulness reaches to the clouds Psalm 36:5 NKJV

LORD your faithful love reaches to heaven, your faithfulness to the clouds. Psalm 36:5 CSB

But you, O Lord, your mercy-seat love is limitless, reaching higher than the highest heavens. Your great faithfulness is infinite, stretching over the whole earth. Psalm 36:5 TPT

One of my male friends since elementary school, the girl he had children with introduced me to heroin when I was almost seventeen. Instantly I was in love, like no love I'd known before. I spent the next two-three years sniffing dope. I didn't know it then, but watching my dad get high for years had planted a seed in me. I wanted to know what he loved so much, what was this thing that kept him from me? I was afraid to shoot up because of the marks it left on my dad, and how it ballooned his hands. One day, I was trying to get as far away from my reality as I could and I did too much and was sick. I threw up everywhere so my home girl told me to mix a little cocaine with it and it would even me out. Here I was mixing heroin and cocaine and ingesting it "speedballin" I was gone. I was living without any regard for my own life. I was getting high and hiding it from my best friend, she wasn't about that life. Weed, cigarettes and drinks were what we were used to. I got high one day and was nodding when this girl was like "I need some of what you had" see, up until then I was getting away with the line "I'm just tired". This same girl later stole some drugs from the Jamaican dudes and they killed her. That's when my best friend realized I was using. I got sick, started throwing up and she began to hit me. She was hurt and crying. Telling me how stupid I was, asking what was wrong with me. I was trying to focus and get myself together, all while trying to block her blows, I heard a voice. It said "you WILL die." I thought it was God. I stopped getting high on heroin and cocaine that day. I told myself I wasn't going to do drugs anymore...that didn't last long, but God's hand remained over me, unknown at the time, He had a plan for my life.

For I know the thoughts that I think toward you, says the Lord, thoughts of peace and not of evil, to give you a future and a hope. Jeremiah 29:11 NKJV

For I know the plans I have for you —-- this is the LORD's declaration —- plans for your well-being, not for disaster, to give you a future and a hope. Jeremiah 29:11 CSB

In all your ways acknowledge Him And He shall direct your paths. Proverbs 3:6 NKJV

In all your ways know him, and he will make your paths straight. Proverbs 3:6 CSB

Become intimate with him in whatever you do, and he will lead you wherever you go.
Proverbs 3:6 TPT

I'd rarely if ever spent money on drugs because everyone I started hanging with either used it or sold it. So I got freebies, for a while anyway. When money became an issue, the guys were more than willing to get me high for free - well, not for free, but the payment wasn't money. It was much more valuable (my body) but at the time It had no worth to me. Now I'm sleeping on dozens of different people's couches, the floor, outside sometimes, wherever I could stay. I had to pull myself together to at least get a job. My first job was at Burger King when I was fourteen, but I didn't work there long because I had to pay my mom rent; she'd take my check, deposit it into her account, and give me about twenty dollars or so. Her words were "Nobody lives for free." When I left her house, I went back and got a job at The Best Western while still hiding from my mom. She had been looking for me ever since I ran away. I only had a little longer to go, I'd be eighteen soon.

Now seventeen, I met a guy from New York. He would come to the hotel when I was working to hang out, really he was waiting for someone bringing drugs on the Peter Pan. The hotel was attached to the Greyhound and Peter Pan bus station. We started spending time together outside the hotel. I was attracted to him because people were afraid of him. I hadn't known anyone like him, he demanded respect and got it. He was a boss. He called the shots. I wasn't afraid of him - at least not in the beginning.

The relationship lasted until I was about twenty, by then I had taken so many beatings and him having other relationships outside of ours, I couldn't count them. I was a prisoner in my own home. I couldn't go anywhere without him or one of his family members. I looked forward to the trips we took on the Peter Pan (greyhound bus) to go to New York to cop (buy drugs) and come back. When I did get to walk to the corner store, I had to have a gun on me or a razor blade in my mouth. He taught me how to give someone a "buck fiddy", that's when you spit a razor from your mouth into someone's face, grab it and take it all the way down to their chin. Guaranteed at least one hundred fifty stitches. Therefore nicknamed "buck 50". Because of the lifestyle we lived, he didn't want to take any chances of someone running up on me and I wasn't prepared to defend myself. His cousin came down from New York, he forgot to tell me he was expecting him, when he knocked on the door and told me who he was, I answered the door with a glock nine pointed at him. I let him inside and told my homegirl to pat him down. "He has a fake leg," she said. He looked at me and said "I got shot and lost my leg" "take it off" I said. He was dumbfounded. "What?" he asked. "take it off!" I repeated. He took his leg off and my homegirl checked it, he was clean. I still held him at gunpoint until my boyfriend came home. He came into the house hours later and burst into laughter. He was laughing and apologizing to him for not telling me he was coming. He liked to test me with situations like that. I'd be driving and he'd say "see the car behind you, (which was usually one of his homeboys) lose it". I'd have to speed in and out of traffic with the car chasing us until I lost it. He made me a getaway driver. It would later come in handy. One night while I was asleep, he covered his face with a ski mask and pretended that he broke into the house to attack me. I woke up fighting, but quickly realized it was him so I stopped fighting. He was extremely upset. "Why didn't you pull out!!?" he shouted. "I knew it was you," I said. We had a real physical fight over a fake situation. He really wanted me to pull my gun on him. It was madness. I lived in a house full of his cousins and friends, along with their girlfriends. We were a house full of battered women, we just didn't know it at the time... we were criminals, all with open court cases, some on the run from other states. I was unfamiliar with the term "battered woman" and would've wanted to fight you if you had called me one to my face. I'd been arrested so many times, in shootouts that I barely escaped with my life, my house was raided multiple times by the police, I was robbed at gunpoint...you name it. Somehow, I always had trust in God even when I didn't have a relationship with Him.

The Lord is good, A stronghold in the day of trouble; And He knows those who trust in Him.

Nahum 1:7 NKJV

The LORD is good, a stronghold in a day of distress; he cares for those who take refuge in him.

Nahum 1:7 CSB

There was one girl I became extremely close to. We were together day in and day out. They'd leave us in the house all day, all night while they were out "handling business" which usually meant they were at thestrip club. My first same-sex encounter was with her. My boyfriend's cousin's girlfriend. One day, my boyfriend and his crew took us to an apartment complex in Dundalk, apparently she had given her number to one of the guys from that complex. We'd been told we were going out to eat and to the movies. We were so excited, we didn't get to go outside...I know, crazy right? We were more than excited. They said we had to stop on the block first, which wasn't unusual since we'd go to pick up money from his workers. We pulled into the apartment complex, got out of the car, and there were two other guys standing there. My dude asked them, "Which one?" pointing at both of us. Now I was totally confused. "Which one?" He asked again. So the guy pointed at her. "She gave me her phone number," he said. I stood there dumbfounded, WHAT??!!? All of a sudden they began to beat her, until she was leaking blood, telling her "you violated" I had to watch helplessly, He wanted to show me what would happen to me if I ever "violated" meaning...talked to or gave another guy my number or disrespected him or his family in any way.

His sister came from New York to live with us. He brought her to Baltimore to save her life, she was doing so much dirt, somebody tried to push her off the roof in New York. I didn't know she had a crack habit. She put some cocaine in a cigarette one day and let me hit it. You know you're not really a crackhead if you smoke it that way...the things we tell ourselves. I was open, I had never felt a rush like that and I wanted to feel it again. "What is that?" I asked her. "A woo" she said. We smoked a couple more, then she said we were wasting the cocaine by smoking it in the cigarette. She made a homemade pipe and we spent the next two days smoking crack. I would steal cocaine from him, he had so much he didn't even know it was missing. I would crawl around on the floor for hours, or clean for hours. One day while cleaning, I found a picture of this naked chic under my bed, and he told me it belonged to his cousin. I thought "yeah ok." My cousin told me it was a girl that worked at a strip club downtown that he was dating. When the relationship was exposed between his cousin's girlfriend and myself, he and I fought violently, and that was my way out. I couldn't do it anymore and neither could he. I wasn't afraid of him anymore and he knew it. I was tired of fighting. I was either going to kill him or he was going to kill me. He told me to get out, so I left, running down the street like Tina Turner ran when she left Ike in the movie What's Love Got To Do With It. I was on my own, with no money and no clothes; he had set them on fire. I had just turned twenty one.

Even though technically we broke up, I wanted to find out about the girl he was seeing. That led me to Baltimore St. "The Block." Nicknamed the block because it's a whole block of strip clubs. I went to the Eldorado's Gentlemen's Club looking for her and walked out with a job. She was off making porn movies. I learned quickly the real money wasn't made dancing inside the club, it was made "dating" outside the club. I became a prostitute...I mean a dancer. I spent the next five years drinking, sniffing dope/coke, popping pills, and self-destructing. I got a call a few months later saying he was murdered in New York. I knew if we'd still been together I would've been with him, he never went to New York without me. God's hand and grace remained over my life even in the worst possible times in my life.

And of His fullness we have all received, and grace for grace. John 1:16 NKJV

Indeed, we have all received grace upon grace from his fullness. John 1:16 CSB

And from the overflow of his fullness we received grace heaped upon more grace. John 1:16 TPT

Let us therefore come boldly to the throne of grace, that we may obtain mercy and find grace to help in time of need.

Hebrews 4:16 NKJV

So now we draw near freely and boldly to where grace is enthroned, to receive mercy's kiss and discover the grace we urgently need to strengthen us in our time of weakness. Hebrews 4:16 TPT

I had attempted suicide three different times in those five years, and was kidnapped and raped by a guy I started dating. He beat and raped me repeatedly for three days and tried to throw me out in the street naked when he was finished with me. I fought like never before, and held clinging by my bloody fingernails to the wall in the vestibule. Finally his aunt came out of her room yelling "enough is enough, leave that girl alone and let her go home before I call the police on you!!" All I remember thinking was...she was in the house the whole time while he was abusing me!!! I couldn't believe she had been there listening to me scream, cry and fight for my life. Things were not the same after that, I guess I had a mental breakdown. I started to feel a tugging from God, again. I wanted to know more about Him even though I was still self medicating, I was still smoking weed and cigarettes, still drinking. I had given up the "hard" stuff.

I met this woman at the strip club where I was working. She was a customer, and we exchanged numbers. I had experienced so much hurt at the hands of guys who claimed to love me, I was longing to be loved, and I remembered how good it felt to be with a female, feeling nurtured. We started a relationship, and a few years in, we exchanged vows with each other, our own personal exchange, before any state recognized same-sex marriage as legal, years before it was ever discussed as being made a law, we had our own personal commitment that meant "marraige" to us.

We, us and her children were all that mattered. Our relationship was good at first, but towards the end, it was filled with jealousy and fighting because I wouldn't stop dancing. I was still sleeping with men for money, I thought that's all they were good for. I couldn't let the money go. She had two small children, and I began to feel convicted about the way we were living in front of them, the relationship, and the violence. I finally walked away one day after a fight that almost cost both of us our lives. I stabbed her after what seemed like an hour long fight because she refused to let me leave. She put a whoopin' on me and I refused to fight back because I felt guilty for cheating. I only picked up the knife to scare her, but it made her more angry. After that, I went with her to the hospital and after talking with the police, who informed me she was refusing medical treatment if they locked me up. That's when I found out I stabbed her within less than half an inch from her lung and she could have died. I made up my mind - no more. I couldn't fight her anymore, I loved her and her children and I didn't want to hurt them anymore. So I made the decision to leave for good.

I started hanging and selling drugs up Park Heights and Belvedere when I wasn't on Monroe and Fayette St. I met a man who was a lot older than me, I was about to turn twenty five. We'd spend days sitting on the block making that money move, and I'd work at the club at night. He was very good to me, but I wasn't used to that, so I didn't know how to receive it. He made sure I was well taken care of. He treated me with respect. He showed me kindness, gentleness. He was getting money when we met but I was getting tired of that life. We'd spend days or weeks in Atlantic City just because we could. I started asking him what he wanted out of life. I felt like there was more to life and we were missing out. I didn't care about the money anymore, I'd seen so much death and backstabbing from so-called friends, I felt like I'd had enough. After really thinking about the question I asked about his life, he left the streets and started working at a local grocery store. He made a plan to pay his way through truck driving school and he executed that plan. He did everything he said he would do and that took his time and his presence away from me. I didn't know how to be alone. I didn't know that I wasn't alone (God was with me). The company he started working for was based out of Minneapolis and he said if we moved there I could see Him more, every night he would be home. I didn't want to move but everything around me was out of control and becoming increasingly more dangerous. My homeboys, guys that I grew up with from elementary...all our lives, committed what was called a "mass murder" unlike anything Baltimore had seen up until then. Killing the family members of other guys we grew up with. It was crazy. So with everything going on around me, I felt like the move might be good for me. I was free to leave, all my court cases for possession were over and my probation had ended. New Year's Eve 1999 I was in a bar in Kenosha Wisconsin. We moved to Minnesota. We didn't have a place right away, so I stayed in a homeless shelter while he went back on the road. I got a job at Mall of America and in about two weeks, we moved into an apartment in Richfield MN. It was good. I needed the change in atmosphere. I was hustling hard, working two jobs... high paying jobs, Supervisor at one, Assistant Manager at the other. I was making good money and I got to keep it all to myself because he paid the bills. He was still on the road all the time and I was left to myself. I met people, made friends, and began hanging out at the clubs. No matter where I am, I can adapt. I met a girl in the club and we started dating . Here I am so far away from home, still bound by the same behaviors I'd tried to leave behind, ever heard the saying "wherever you go, there you are"? In Minnesota for three years barely seeing him, mixed up with the wrong crowd, it didn't matter where I was, I always migrated to the "wrong crowd". The girl I was seeing decided she wanted to have "fun" and try some cocaine, I thought, why not? I remembered the fun I used to have being high and carefree. Isn't it something how the enemy will cause you to remember something that almost killed you and you remember it as "fun". After months of getting high with her, it had run its course. I was done with getting high (again) we'd spent three days smoking crack and I asked God if He'd let me come down off that high, I wouldn't get high anymore. I was missing my family. No matter how dysfunctional I thought they were, I missed them so much and I wanted to see them. Besides, dysfunction was my normal, and I missed it. I love them. I made arrangements to get back to Baltimore and left Minnesota and all I owned. It was 2003, the girl I spent years in a relationship with sent me money to get the bus back to Baltimore. I left that man who had been nothing but good to me because I wanted and needed him physically there with me and he couldn't be. My Boogaloo. I wasn't mature enough or healed enough to understand he was doing what he had to do to provide for us. The best he could. He said to me "nice guys always finish last, but they finish" I didn't understand how blessed I was to have him, So in my neediness, I hooked up with the guy I would ultimately have my first four children with. The guy I'd known since he was twelve. My mother and his father had been married but were now divorced. For years while they were married he and I were very close. We had the best relationship / friendship. That changed when I gave birth to his children.

The Start of the Journey From Darkness to Light

When I became pregnant with my first daughter, I was just about to turn thirty. Before I got pregnant I had decided to change my life. I didn't realize that meant submitting to God, I tried it on my own, taking things into my own hands. I wanted to settle down, I had stopped drinking and partying. It started out good, but that was the start of another painful addiction. He became my addiction; we had a very abusive relationship, like all the other relationships I had (except one) but this time I was the abuser most of the time. We had three children and one on the way, and he thought three children was enough, so he asked me to abort my fourth baby. He didn't know I was still scarred and haunted by the faces of the two children I had aborted when I was fourteen, so that wasn't even an option for me. He was much younger than I, and he felt like he didn't want any more children. Having children made our relationship even more stressful, so he left me when I told him I wouldn't have an abortion.

No one had ever left me before. I always did the leaving, it was always me who ended a relationship, so when he left me, it was a mental shock. A few weeks before he left, we fought and we're both arrested. I'm pregnant in jail feeling like the ultimate failure. It was the second fight we'd had and we're both arrested for. When we got out of jail, he left and a big part of me (my sanity) went with him. I'd always imagined having children, a family, but never being a single mom. I was emotionally and mentally crippled, unable to stand. After my first daughter was born, he left. I'd talked to his mom in Tobago and she told me he was planning on going there to visit. I explained to her that he'd left me. She was heartbroken, after I sold all I could...everything I owned of value...and his mom helped me get to Trinidad and

Tobago. It was to no avail. I lived there for eight months and still came back to the states without him, so my second daughter wouldn't be born in Tobago and not have citizenship in America. He didn't want us. She was born not long after my release from jail. Coming back to America, I was arrested at Dulles Airport because I missed a court date from an arrest early in the year, A previous fight with him. So when my passport was scanned at the airport, it read: FUGITIVE FLED FROM JUSTICE. I spent a week in jail praying my daughter would not be born in jail and taken away from me. God allowed her to come almost a week after my release. She was born and three days after we were home, I was preparing to take her to her well-child check-up. I fed her and watched the color leave, literally drain out of her face. In a panic I shook her, not hard, but enough to get her back. I yelled for my mom (I was back with my mom). We took her to the doctors and it happened again, several times. They couldn't understand what was happening. They escorted us by ambulance from the clinic to Johns Hopkins Hospital where she underwent every test imaginable. Her heart stopped repeatedly. They went through every family disease. I had to call her dad in Tobago and ask his family if they had any family diseases that I didn't know about. Finally they called in a specialist and he came to speak with me. He said he had an idea of what he thought the problem was and he wanted to test it to be sure. He asked if I had acid reflux when I was pregnant with her. I did. The worst case of it, it was absolutely terrible. The doctor did his test, and sure enough after she ate, she stopped breathing. She had acid reflux, and it was clogging her airway when she finished eating. She had spent a week in ICU and we now knew what the culprit was. She had to be fed through a tube inserted in her nose into her stomach and put on medication for months. Fast forward, now three kids in and one on the way. The enemy wanted me to believe I couldn't take care of my children without him, even though he wasn't a provider. I found myself back in suicide mode, thinking my children would be better off without me, I had nothing to offer them, at times, not even a home. My oldest two daughters and I had lived in the car for a little while after my mom and I got into a heated argument about a storage bill she said she would pay for me while I was gone. All I didn't sell went into storage when I left for Tobago. I got a call from the storage place saying my things were going to be auctioned off unless I made the full payment to stop the auction. I didn't have the money. When I reminded her she said she would pay the storage bill for me, she was furious. The argument made her put us out. We were now homeless because nobody had "room" for us, and the enemy was taunting me about that.

"It shall come to pass That before they call, I will answer; And while they are still speaking, I will hear." Isaiah 65:24 NKJV

Even before they call, I will answer, while they are still speaking I will hear. Isaiah 65:24 CSB

I had brought a lil piece of car from my uncle's friend and I would drop off my daughters with my aunt in the morning and give people rides all day to make enough money to get a motel room for the night. During this time, I was in therapy at Johns Hopkins for severe depression, "Major Depressive Disorder," in their terms. See, unresolved trauma has many names, many faces. My therapist helped us get housing, but I couldn't seem to think straight. I couldn't talk without crying. I was in the deepest, darkest place inside myself. I was full of self-hatred. I was pleading with him to come back to us, but he wouldn't. He would come back to sleep with me and leave again. I ran into an old boyfriend and in a week, we were married. I did it to make my children's father jealous. He didn't care. We were immediately divorced. As a matter of fact, he didn't even make it back to my house after the ceremony. He'd been living with the mother of his daughter and had to go there to get his clothes. When he went into the house, I drove off. It was a whole mess. He kept calling asking me to come back and get him but I knew it wasn't the right thing to do. It goes to show where my mental state was. I had tried "church" before but went back to the streets where I knew more, and was more comfortable. The pain inside me was unbearable. I couldn't be, nor did I want to be, in my own skin. The enemy was tormenting me mentally, daily, all day, Everyday.

All at once, my mind replayed my encounters with every man and woman I had willingly and unwillingly given myself to sexually, and I hated it. I felt ashamed. Thinking one day my children would know who I once was and what I had been, and still may be, because I couldn't get free from the thoughts and feelings. So, at what I thought was my end...I said a prayer to God, to forgive me for what I was about to do to myself, my children, and my family. I prayed for forgiveness and prepared to end my life. I opened the door so the police didn't have to break it down to free my children, and there was a lady walking up to my porch about to knock on my door. I was quickly ready to dismiss her, I thought she was selling something, I said "whatever you're selling, I don't want it" when she asked, "Do you know that Jesus died for you?" I knew it was God telling me Jesus had already died for me so I didn't have to take my life. I fell to my knees, weeping at this woman's feet. I knew God had sent an angel at the very moment I was planning to commit suicide.

Sing, O heavens! Be joyful, O earth! And break out singing, O mountains! For the Lord has comforted His people, And will have mercy on His afflicted. Isaiah 49:13 NKJV

Shout for joy, you heavens! Earth, rejoice! Mountains break into joyful shouts! For the LORD has comforted his people, and will have compassion on the afflicted ones. Isaiah 49:13 CSB

She invited me to her church. I attended that Sunday with my children, August 20, 2006. I accepted Jesus Christ as my Lord and Savior and was baptized that day. I had tried church before, but not Jesus. God began a work in and through me. I attended church regularly, and a class on Friday nights to help people struggling with strongholds. When I started attending, someone at the church gifted me the workbooks I needed for the class. I started doing my weekly lessons. One lesson in the book asked me to write my testimony. I began to tell my story of this gun toting, dope sniffing prostitute who struggled with homosexuality, depression, suicide attempts, homelessness, rape, multiple arrests etc...When I got to my teenage years, it began with my first boyfriend. I started thinking about him. Where was he? How was he doing? Last I had heard, he had twenty five years for attempted murder. After discussing it with my girlfriend she told me about this online site where you could find people who were locked up, with one click, I found him. There in front of me on the computer screen was the name of the facility that housed him along with his inmate number. Remember I said the enemy will cause you to remember the good times about a situation and not the bad.

I just stared at it for a while, then I wrote it down, tried to gather my thoughts, and began to write him a letter. I told him all that I'd been through since we'd broken up. Oddly enough, I didn't remember why we'd broken up. After pouring my heart out in about 5 pages, I felt like I'd overwhelm him with all that, I thought I'd better keep it simple. I tore up the letter and wrote another one - a much shorter one. I kept attending church, but didn't hear from him. It never dawned on me to ask God if I should write to him, or if I was making the right decision. I was still leading myself. My mom would say...it was the blind leading the blind. It took almost a month for me to receive a letter from him. I didn't know it, but at the time I had sent my letter, he was being transferred to a Baltimore City facility from Cumberland. He had spent years there, fifteen to be exact. I found out later he was in the same prison with the man who murdered my father in 1994.

I didn't officially know my father was dead until 2000. While living in Minnesota I was contacted by a State's Attorney with the Baltimore City State's Attorney's Office. I had known in my heart, though; my dad had lived two places his whole life, either with my grandmother or my grandfather. When he was neither of those places after about a week, I knew something had to have happened to him. She asked if she could fly me back to Baltimore to testify about the last conversation I had with my dad. My dad had told me he'd accepted a package of heroin from his girlfriend's brother and he used more than he sold and he owed this guy a lot of money. He wanted me to ask my boyfriend at the time for some money so he could pay the guy back, but I was afraid to ask. My boyfriend was much more dangerous than this guy my dad owed money to. When I finally got up the nerve to ask, it was too late. The guy my dad owed the money to came up with a scheme that they would rob a jewelry store in Baltimore County. They'd watched the place for a while and thought they could rob the owner while he was transporting the money from the jewelry store to the bank. Things went wrong, horribly wrong. There was a shootout and my father was shot in the neck. Instead of taking him to the hospital, they took him somewhere isolated and killed him. His body was never recovered. The stolen van used to commit the crime was recovered. There was enough blood in the van to test his DNA which they collected from my grandmother, myself and his siblings. It was a match. They knew from the amount of blood, he couldn't have survived. Crazy thing is, my father was listed as a missing person for years and the Baltimore City police didn't search for him. It was two Baltimore County Homicide Detectives that looked into the case after a man was arrested on an unrelated charge and asked to speak to Homicide Detectives. He wanted to make a deal to get out of jail. He told the Detectives about a murder that no one knew about...he tried to tell the story as if he'd heard about it from other jailers talking. They didn't have any hospital or police reports to support the story and so they began backtracking in an attempt to locate my father. What stood out to the detectives was my father had an arrest record dating back to 1974. Every year since 1974 he had been arrested for something. His arrest record stopped in May of 1994. The detectives pieced together the crime from the story the inmate told them, tracked down what evidence they could, and came to us with the story. They called it, as did the newspapers, a botched robbery. My father had been murdered by his girlfriend's brother, and his body, to this day, has never been found. It was the first case in Maryland where a man was convicted of murder without a body. I don't have words to describe what I felt.

Let, I pray Your merciful kindness be for my comfort, According to Your word to Your servant. Psalm 119:76 NKJV

May your faithful love comfort me as you promised your servant. Psalm 119:76 CSB

Send your kind mercy-kiss to comfort me, your servant, just like you promised you would.

Psalm 119:76 TPT

Because he (my ex), my very first boyfriend, was being transferred to a different facility my letter reached the former place, and had to be sent to the new facility where he was being housed, so it took some time to reach him. When he received my letter, he wrote me back. I remember standing there looking at the little white envelope with so much excitement. His handwriting still looked exactly the same. I hadn't heard from him since we were sixteen and I was now thirty-four. Excited, I went to open the letter and heard a voice in my ear, "He's going to bring death to you." WHAT?!!?? I got angry, "Why is my thinking so jacked up?" I asked myself. I didn't know it at the time, but it was the Holy Spirit speaking to me, and because I didn't discern the voice I heard, I thought it was my voice I heard. I knew absolutely nothing about discernment. I immediately dismissed the thought, I was so happy to see his name on that envelope. When I opened the letter and read it, I was all the more excited. He expressed how much he missed me and had always kept tabs on me over the years, how much he still loved me, all the things I so desperately wanted to hear. I was elated. He said he'd be home in a few months, and when he came home he wanted to see me. I'd already let him know in my letter I was in church and at a place in my life where I wouldn't play house with anybody. I had stopped smoking weed and cigarettes, stopped drinking, partying, everything was different now. I wanted a clean start, a fresh start. He told me he found the Lord while in prison and he wanted the same things I wanted, what God wanted. When I wrote him back and gave him my number, he called and asked me to marry him. I thought, let's be real, you don't want to marry me, you want to move in and play house and I'm not with that. I had three children, and was pregnant with my fourth. He was persistent however, every time we'd talk, he'd say, "You know you're going to be my wife. I'm not going to lose you again." I was giddy, I can't lie. After much discussion, I thought, He's really not playing, he wants to marry me and so I accepted his proposal, without talking to my Heavenly Father, without praying, fasting, seeking wise counsel...I agreed. YES!!! I'm getting married!!!!

He told his mom and she called me so she could come by for dinner one evening. We were both so happy. "This has to be from God" she said "only God could reunite you two after all these years." I was in total agreement with her, my common sense didn't say...actually, I looked him up online. I didn't talk to God about it at all. But, I didn't say that to her. She met my children, we talked, laughed, cried, and got caught up with each other's lives.

So, it was official! I was getting married! I was active in the women's group at my church, and I shared the news of my engagement with them and it wasn't well received. I remember the negative comments from some of the women there, which upset me. The nerve! I thought. It wasn't well received by a lot of people, but did I care? Nope. Not at all. Finally on his way home upon his release, he asked me to pick up a bottle of Grey Goose (vodka) for him to celebrate coming home. That was surely a red flag I overlooked. I didn't want to get it, I'd stopped drinking a year prior. I should've stood my ground and said, "Grey who? I don't drink, and I'm not buying liquor." It is when we don't hold ourselves to God's standards, we make our own.

Looking back, I handicapped him from the start. Everything he needed, I bought for him, down to his socks. I was helping him get on his feet, so I didn't see a problem with it. I remember standing outside the jail for hours waiting for him to walk out of the door. When he finally came out, his mom began to scream and thank God. We laughed and cried. When we got home, he took off the state's clothes, showered, got dressed, and to the courthouse we went. Just like that, bam! I am married now! When the ceremony was over, we returned home. He had a McDonald's sweet tea cup, he poured cup after cup of Grey Goose, I really didn't know how much he was drinking; I was trying not to notice. Before I knew it, I had to help him upstairs into the bathroom. He was extremely sick - so intoxicated, that I thought he had alcohol poisoning. I got him into the bedroom, and he passed out on the bed until the next day. I was thinking to myself, really dude!! I felt like I'd made a terrible mistake but I was unwilling to admit it. Unwilling to hear the "I told you so" speeches that I knew I'd hear. I was afraid to be seen as a failure.

For God has not given us a spirit of fear, but of power and love and of a strong mind

2 Timothy 1:7 NKJV

For God has not given us a spirit of fear, but one of power, love and sound judgment

2 Timothy 1:7 CSB

For God will never give you the spirit of fear, but the Holy Spirit who gives you mighty power, love, and self-control. 2 Timothy 1:7 TPT

I was mad at myself for buying the liquor. Oh, but me being "Pleasing Patty," it wouldn't be the last liquor I would buy. Even though I was uncomfortable with It, I was too afraid to say no so I did whatever he asked, even though I knew better. I was being convicted about it, and I learned to live with the conviction, as uncomfortable as that is. Slowly, over time, I began to drink with him, and starting smoking cigarettes and weed again. About a year passed before I found out I was pregnant with our first child together. I prayed so hard for her; I felt guilty having four children, and none by my husband. I was in a rush to have his baby; I took a pregnancy test every week. He was laughing at me. Then one day...POSITIVE... I was so exceedingly happy. I didn't even stop to think, I'm having my fifth child, and he's not even working. I mean, there was not a thought of fear or worry, just excitement. People thought I was crazy. Maybe I was, but I believed we were supposed to have a lot of children, so why not? We were married. My mother called me every stupid so and so she could think of.

I quit smoking and drinking while I was pregnant, and each time, I would feel like, This is it, I'm not going back to that. After giving birth, I would look at him, because of what he was doing, I would feel like, ok, why am I trying to be a miss goody goody?" It wasn't really about what he was doing at all. I had unhealed hurt and trauma that I spent years avoiding and trying to bandage on my own. My relationship (or lack of) with God had taken a back seat, due to the overwhelming feelings of guilt and shame. Me being me, I was doing my own thing yet again. Everything started to spiral out of control in an instant it seemed like. I was condemning myself, I felt like God was through with me.

For I am persuaded that neither death nor life, nor angels nor principalities nor powers nor things present nor things to come, nor height nor depth, nor any other created thing, shall be able to separate us from the love of God which is in Christ Jesus our Lord. Romans 8:38-39 NKJV

So now I live with the confidence that there is nothing in the universe with the power to separate us from God's love. I'm convinced that his love will triumph over death, life's troubles, fallen angels, or dark rulers in the heavens. There is nothing in our present or future circumstances that can weaken his love. There is no power above or beneath us - no power that could ever be found in the universe that can distance us from God's passionate love, which is lavished upon us through our Lord Jesus, the Anointed One. Romans 8:38-39 TPT

One day, this young guy knocked on my door and asked me for a dime bag. A what!!? Excuse me!!? I yelled. He said the big dude that lived here told him he had weed for sale. I told him there was nothing for sale and he'd better not knock on my door again.. After that, I was telling more and more people not to knock on my door. I cursed my husband out, "Why would you tell people to come knock on the door where we live!!!?" I screamed. "Now you're selling weed out of our house?!!!!?"

He said he told them to see him when he was outside. He'd given one of the teenagers in the neighborhood a pound of weed that was given to him by one of his homeboys as a welcome home present. He was angry, saying this little boy better have his money. Sooooo I'm like, first of all, where did you get a pound of weed? Second, you just came home, you don't even know the boy down the street, so you basically handed a pound of weed to a dude you don't even know, and you're waiting for him to bring you some money back...(If I could insert an emoji here, it would be the one with the lady holding her head) I didn't even have the words. Needless to say I started looking for a new place to live because I wasn't comfortable in my home anymore. I wanted to get as far away from that neighborhood as I could. I didn't see it or know it at the time, but God was still working it out for my good. His hand remained; even in my unfaithfulness, He favored me. I didn't know why, but He did. God had given me visions when I was about twelve or thirteen. He showed me myself...singing in this big beautiful place. I'd never been there or seen it before. But I saw it in my vision.

Breaking the Concrete Around My Heart

I moved from Baltimore to PG County in 2008. Starting over. I had to lay down some rules. House rules. There would be no foolishness allowed. PA HA!! I guess that's what he was thinking. I'd already allowed it for a year, now I'm laying down rules, putting my foot down. Yeah, ok. We began going to church, active in the church, children in their classes, learning bible stories, everything seemingly going good. Did I mention I had another baby? For a brief time while waiting for the house in PG to be ready we had to move in with my sister for almost a month and a half, still in Baltimore. That didn't go too well, we'd end up arguing over a seven hundred dollar BGE bill which I was convinced was more than a month's worth of BGE. Anyway, that started an argument between her and I that my mom got involved in, my mom, always getting involved to curse me out, it was the two of them against me. That really prompted me to search for a house far away from them. We had to leave my sister's house and live in a motel for almost a month while waiting for the house in PG County. Eight of us in a motel room. We finally moved to Clinton Maryland. Far enough away where no one would just show up without calling. The same month we moved, my mom called, and the conversation went something like this..."My doctor wants me to have some tests done. I'm not worried about it, and you shouldn't be either" she said very nonchalantly.

In 2003, after I had my first child, she'd been diagnosed with breast cancer, but they weren't worried because they caught it early, while it was small. They had gone in and taken it out, and it was gone. Then, almost five years later, approaching her five year celebration of being cancer-free "It's nothing to worry about " she said. She had been complaining for months of severe pain in her arms and legs. "It feels like someone has beat me with a bat in my sleep" she'd say. I'd been in a backslidden state for quite some time and my heart was hard. Very hard. I really didn't care, at least I didn't think I cared. After consistently complaining to her doctor, he sent her to have a bone scan done. We found out she had stage four metastatic breast cancer. I can remember thinking, That's what she gets. Am I supposed to care? That's what my mind said but really I was broken. I had lived with the hurt and anger for so long, feeling betrayed by her, unwanted by her, unloved. I thought...I really thought I don't care either way. I didn't allow myself to feel. I tried not to feel, but I was wrong. I was used to giving the enemy what he wanted, letting him control my emotions, letting him feed and thrive off my anger and bitterness. That had been my way for many years. I had put up concrete walls around my heart. I thought I was shielding my heart from hurt and pain but I was shielding it from love, God's love. I was hurt by repeated infidelity in my marriage, but decided to stay because I wanted my children to have a family with both parents. I thought I was doing what was best for them. I kept excusing his behavior because he'd spent so much time in prison. I thought I was being a good wife by staying by his side. Things in my marriage went from bad to worse, but I hung in there. My heart was so heavy and full of pain, my mind full of negativity, I was self medicating again, just to cope. My mother lived seven years in stage four. She received chemo the whole time, had several radiation treatments and brain surgery to remove a tumor. We were told that she would appear to have had a stroke, but she didn't miss a beat. Her speech was not slurred, her face did not slant, nothing. If it hadn't been for the scar, you wouldn't have known she had brain surgery. I was so emotionally drained. I tried to put on a happy face, but I felt like I was dying inside. I began to get angry with God. Where was He? I had the nerve to holler and scream at Him. WHY ARE YOU DOING THIS TO ME?!!!!!? HAVEN'T I SUFFERED ENOUGH?!!!!!!? I felt like I wanted to die... I. Literally. Wanted. To. Die.

For years, I struggled with suicide; I couldn't find happiness. I didn't realize I was actually looking for joy...and only God can give it. Even being a mom, the one thing I always wanted to be (beside a wife) I felt like I was failing at it. I'd pick myself apart: I wasn't this, I don't have that, I'm not the right shape... all the lies the enemy wanted me to believe, I believed. Seven years. SEVEN YEARS! Stage four Metastatic Breast Cancer. WAIT!! WHAT!!? She didn't look sick. The whole time, she looked so good, as beautiful as ever. She still went out all the time, and refused to sit still. She had a Karaoke calendar so she knew where Karaoke was every day of the week. She was a songbird. "Sultry songstress" she nicknamed herself. She was in such good shape, always looking flawless, I never really made the connection. I never allowed my mind to process the diagnosis. I'd heard the words "stage 4 cancer" but because she didn't look sick, because of my hardened heart, I put it out of my mind. Her last three months of life, that's when it became evident to me. One day I looked at her, she had lost about 20 pounds seemingly overnight. Things started to look bad. I could physically see the changes. Up until then, I would have people say to me... I saw your mom, she looks beautiful, I thought she was sick, someone told me she has cancer. Those last three months, I wish those images would leave my memory, I will never forget those images. I had never been to treatment with her and decided I should go after she broke down on the phone one day about being the only one at treatment alone. "Everyone has someone there with them except me" she said. My sister and I begin to alternate days, she'd go one day, then I'd go the next. Meeting her Oncologist, the doctors talked us through what had been their treatment plan and explained to us that they'd given her the most aggressive Chemo in the very beginning and there was simply nothing else they could do. It was hearing those words that made everything real to me, made my heart feel. Nothing. Else. We. Can. Do. I started asking questions, I wanted there to be something else they could do. I wouldn't accept that as an answer. At that moment, I saw my mom. I mean really saw her. Her once vibrant glowing skin was dull and pale. She'd lost so much weight, she was almost unrecognizable. She looked like she was twice her age. After giving us the "nothing else they can do" speech, they recommended Hospice, giving her a few months to live. They said she could no longer live on her own. Though she looked frail, she was still in her right mind and didn't want to go into a Hospice facility. She refused to go and I refused to send her. After a week-long back and forth exchange, she agreed to come live with us. Hospice care came to my house throughout the week for a few hours to care for her. I promised her it would only be a short stay and when she got stronger she could return to her apartment. She agreed, but he didn't get stronger, everyday she got weaker. Crazy thing is, my children don't seem to remember her before the cancer took over. I show them pictures and they are in awe. It was discussed that I should consider putting her in hospice when the time came, but there was no way I could do that. As the end approached, she would always say, "Just let me go to the hospital for a few days." As soon as she'd get there, she would want to come home. She was so afraid. I was praying with and for her. One day I was praying and the Holy Spirit spoke to me, and said my mom was going to die - His exact words were "Your mom is going to die, and so is your marriage." My prayer had been for a miracle. "Heal her Lord, only You can." He reminded me that His will would be done and not mine. "We have so much to fix," I said. We had never resolved the issues we had for years over the molestation, the abortion, the anger and bitterness. I thought, how unfair. I never got to say how bad it (she) hurt me, she never said sorry. She was wrong! Now I have to act like nothing ever happened? All is forgiven? Well it's not! I didn't know how. I was devastated. She owed me an apology. She was supposed to be there for me, my dad wasn't around and I needed her. Being her caregiver became so overwhelming. She didn't trust the Hospice nurses so it was a full-time hands on job for me. I had spent the majority of my life in self destruct mode because of brokenness and trauma surrounding the sexual abuse, and now, just forget about it? HOW?!!! I! Don't! Know! How! I still took care of her, I loved her and I wanted her to get well. I wanted her healed. My mom and my sister were much closer than my mom and I, they always were, and if you had asked her who she would rather live with, she would have said my sister for sure.

My sister suffered a mental breakdown as my mother's cancer got worse. She couldn't deal with my mom's diagnosis or her rapidly changing appearance. I was running back and forth to Baltimore to help look after my sister and her daughter when I could. The Oncologist said they'd given her (my mom) everything they could, even experimental drugs that turned her hands and feet black like charcoal. It got to the point she could no longer drive, eat, or walk on her own. I had to assist her with everything. She kept complaining of stomach pain and had to be taken to the hospital where they pumped liters of what looked like liquid charcoal from her stomach. I kept asking the doctors what the black liquid was but no one would give me an answer. On her last day of walking, four days before she died, I helped her into bed, and she just stared at me. The longest stare I ever remember from her, then she said, with the faintest voice "I'm sorry for EVERYTHING" It was the way she said "everything" I knew what she was talking about. I told her there was nothing to be sorry about. I thought to myself, I waited all these years to hear those words, and they didn't change anything. I didn't feel better. It didn't take my pain away. I just wanted her to get well. I couldn't stand seeing her frail and helpless. I would lay in bed beside her and read the bible, sing, pray, kiss her cheek, rub her hands and her head that was now completely bald. She looked like a skeleton with skin. Literally, a skeleton with skin. Being a wife, her full-time caregiver and mother of eight was taking a toll on me, but God! He literally had angels holding me up. Angels that sometimes came in the form of human sisters and their husbands who wrapped their loving arms around us and carried me when I couldn't walk, but I could crawl. So I crawled, with them holding my arms, I crawled. They brought us food some days, some of my ministry sisters would come sit with me, or come over and say "Marilyn go take a drive".

But those who wait on the Lord Shall renew their strength; They shall mount up with wings like eagles, They shall run and not be weary, They shall walk and not faint.

Isaiah 40:31 NKJV

But those who trust in the LORD will renew their strength; they will soar on wings like eagles; they will run and not become weary, they will walk and not faint. Isaiah 40:31 CSB

The days passed and it was torture to watch her barely breathe, not able to eat. I knew she wouldn't survive long without eating so I pleaded with Hospice to insert a feeding tube in her but they explained in her weak feeble state she wouldn't survive surgery. It had to be three or four days of listening to the gurgling, her struggling to breathe, too weak to swallow. I did my best to suction her mouth. I'll never forget the sound or the look of death, the smell. I was pleading with God to please take her. My prayer went from please save her to please take her. My sister and aunt had been to my house and had left to go to the store.

When they got back from the store, my sister came and laid beside her, sobbing and saying "it's ok ma, you can go. I'll be ok". I had spent days saying these words to her but she needed to hear them from my sister. Then the gurgling stopped. There, in the guest room, the room she claimed as hers years before when I moved into the house. It was quiet. After a long exhale from her, it was silent. I didn't even realize how broken I was until my mother died, and then I realized that while I was going through the motions of life, trying to be what and who my family needed me to be, I had not forgiven her, truly forgiven her. In my heart. The pain I felt was so unimaginable, I can't even articulate it. I thought I couldn't possibly hurt anymore than I already did. Why didn't I say anything years ago so we could move past all this? Why had I wasted all those years, time spent being angry? Why this, and why that? I was tormented with pain, guilt and regret. At the time of her death, I was in a discipleship class at my new church First Baptist Church of Glenarden, Queen Esther. An eighteen month class that disciples women and teaches them to build and to seek a closer relationship with God. Being in the class began to peel back layers of "stuff" that was buried so deep inside me and needed to be uprooted. I found through that class the pathway to begin to heal. I was in a class with twenty-two women and we were all, to one another, who we needed in that season. We helped each other through our trials while learning to lean on God's Word. We learned the truth about who we are in Him. The beautiful blessing is that it also built a life-long sisterhood between us. God's hand and love is ever faithful, and it remained, His presence remained with me and

Unless the LORD had been my help, My soul would soon have settled in silence.

Psalm 94:17 NKJV

If the Lord had not been my helper, I would soon rest in the silence of death. Psalm 94:17 CSB

I would have been killed so many times if you had not been there for me. Psalm 94:17 TPT

He continued strengthening me and allowing me grace to get through each day, and please understand...I needed His grace every second of every day. Not even a month after my mom passed, my husband moved out (again) over a ten year period, it became a regular event, so regular my children weren't moved by it anymore. He found something to get upset about and went in on me, telling me I'm the cancer and I'm killing him, I'm the reason he wasn't doing well in life because I was suffocating him, everytime he got a "decent" job, I'd get sick and have to go to the hospital and he'd have to stay with our children. He told me I was going to die sick and alone just like my mom. That was it. I was done. I didn't care anymore if he stayed or left. I didn't and couldn't couldn't cry anymore. GO!! GET OUT!!! PLEASE!!! THIS TIME DON'T COME BACK!!! I was emotionally drained, I was exhausted, I was empty. This time, I wasn't crying, calling, texting or pleading for "my family". He had moved out so many times before, leaving me with our children. I was used to being a single parent, even while married. With the help and support of the QE director, my facilitators and sisters in my class, I graduated from Queen Esther a few weeks before and I was trying to build a closer relationship with God. I was learning to trust Him and depend on Him. Every thought, every need, I laid at His feet.

When he left, the enemy tried again to convince me that I shouldn't be with a man. That's where the pain in my life started, and I shouldn't keep trying to make it work with a man, but for the sake of my children, and my relationship with God, I would. I did. I've raised my children in the church; they've been taught what the bible says about homosexuality, and so have I. I didn't want to live a life contrary to the bible in front of my children. I didn't have peace about it. However, I was still entertaining the thought. Maybe God wouldn't care because He knew what I'd suffered at the hands of men. The Holy Spirit would not leave me alone, He kept reminding me God called me out of that lifestyle. I had my mind made up thinking we were going to get a divorce, but I prayed and after his constant pleading, I put the thought aside and decided to try to save my marriage. After many, many trials, we made it over the hump, through all the good, the bad, and the ugly - we made it. Ten years.

Every couple of months for the past couple of years, I'd have to be admitted to the hospital, due to my blood pressure. It would be so high my eyes felt like they were going to pop out of the sockets. On more than one occasion the EMT said he had never seen a blood pressure so high without the person having a stroke. I'd been diagnosed with CHF (Congestive Heart Failure) in 2010 after I had my last child, and ever since then had been back and forth for years with either heart or blood pressure issues. My last stay in the hospital would be life changing. Drastically. November 15, 2015. I was transported to Southern Maryland Hospital by ambulance. That night, like so many others, I was admitted, I got a text that my younger cousin had died. I couldn't believe what I was reading, it read "she has left this life" she was the fourth younger cousin I had lost. I cried and cried. My last conversation with her I promised I would return to the nursing home where she was to spend time with her. I didn't get the chance.

It was my second day in Southern Md hospital when I received a call from Child Protective Services, first thing in the morning. The woman on the other end of the phone told me who she was and kept repeating she didn't want to upset me because she knew I was in the hospital. I didn't understand what she was trying to say. She told me my oldest daughter had gone to school and said my husband, her dad for the last ten years, tried to have sex with her the night before. He asked her to have sex with him, were her exact words. WHAT?!!? It was like she was speaking a foreign language. I was stunned and confused. To be honest, I was angry. I felt like I had to make myself take a breath. I was told by the woman not to say anything to him until they could talk to him about it...WHAT!!??? ARE YOU CRAZY??? She told me he would have to leave the house pending an investigation and if he didn't leave the house, Child Protective Services would remove all my children from my home until I was released from the hospital. As soon as I hung up the phone with her, I called my sister in Baltimore.

I told my sister what happened, and she and her fiancé came right away. I tried to get my thoughts together before I called him, but I couldn't. I called him and told him he needed to come to the hospital. When he got there, I asked him what happened between him and my oldest daughter. He looked confused. "nothing," he said. "SOMETHING!!" I said. Then he said, "oh yeah, she had to get a spanking last night." I remembered calling him that night and he hadn't answered. That was odd. He hadn't answered, or called me back. His reason was that he fell asleep. That was strange, but for me to fathom he could or would do the unthinkable, my mind could not, would not process that. He said she was using her tablet. She wasn't supposed to be using it because she was punished so he spanked her. He said he told her to pull her pants down and she did, then he pulled her underwear down, made her lay on his lap and spanked her. A part of my mind shut down. Why did you tell her to pull her pants down!!?? Why did she have to pull her underwear down!!?? She's 12!!!! You never spanked her like that before!!! I was furious. He got angry with me. "I'm her father!" he yelled. Why are you questioning me!!? "You need to find out why she's lying and trying to ruin my life," he said. Because of the accusation, he had to move out. He moved with his aunt in Baltimore. I was distraught.

I, even I, am He who comforts you. Isaiah 51:12 NKJV

I - I am the one who comforts you. Who are you that you should fear humans who die, or a son of man who is given up like grass? Isaiah 51:12 CSB

CPS began their investigation and he maintained his innocence. He told me he was praying God would reveal the truth, those were his words. He's praying God will reveal the truth. He started texting me prayers and scriptures everyday. He had been a witness to what God was doing in me, the pursuit of me. God pursued me and he was there to watch my transformation. He told me the enemy was using my daughter to tear our family apart. All I could do was pray because I didn't know who to believe. This was one of the worst times in my life, besides my parents dying, my molestation, rape, worse because I felt I had to choose between my husband and my daughter.

I'd been through some pretty awful stuff in life, beaten and raped by acquaintances and boyfriends, sexual abuse, domestic violence, almost stangled to death more than once, nearly overdosed on heroin and I felt this hurt was a different level of pain. This was my breaking point. I was knocked down, in every way, mentally and emotionally. I couldn't physically get up to do anything, I was a wreck. I kept praying. CPS concluded their investigation and couldn't determine what - if anything had happened because there was no DNA evidence. She said he "asked" her to have sex with him. He was denying it so their investigation ended as UNDETERMINED. It was a he says / she says case, so they put a safety plan in place that would allow him to come back in the house with me being present at all times. He had spent months convincing me my daughter was lying on him, and I believed him. "The devil is trying to tear our family apart" he kept saying. He was still living with his aunt after they closed the case and he made me feel horrible for ever thinking he would do something like that. Once the investigation was closed, he immediately asked if he could come back home, but I felt uneasy, my spirit wouldn't rest. I was torn. I didn't know which way to go...what to believe. I couldn't understand, knowing that she loved him dearly, why would she say that? Why? Was she that angry for being punished that she would lie like that? Is she at the age where she's starting to rebel because of her lack of relationship with her biological father? I don't know! HELP ME JESUS!!! Everyday. Everyday. EVERYDAY!! I cried, GOD PLEASE HELP ME!!!

In the day when I cried out, You answered me, and made me bold with strength in my soul.

Psalm 138:3 NKJV

On the day I called, you answered me; you increased strength within me. Psalm 138:3 CSB

At the very moment I called out to you, you answered me! You strengthened my soul and breathed fresh courage into me. Psalm 138:3 TPT

Though the Lord is on high, yet He regards the lowly. Though I walk in the midst of trouble, You will revive me; You will stretch out Your hand against the wrath of my enemies, and Your right hand will save me. The Lord will perfect that which concerns me;

Your mercy O Lord, endures forever; do not forsake the work of Your hands.

Psalm 138:6-8 NKJV

Though the Lord is exalted, he takes note of the humble; but he knows the haughty from a distance. If I walk into the thick of danger, you will preserve my life from the anger of my enemies. You will extend your hand; your right hand will save me. Lord your faithful love endures forever; do not abandon the work of your hands. Psalm

138:6-8 CSB

For though you are lofty and exalted, you stoop to embrace the lowly. Yet you keep your distance from those filled with pride. By your mighty power I can walk through any devastation, and you will keep me alive, reviving me. Your power set me free from the hatred of my enemies. You keep every promise you've ever made to me! Since your love for me is constant and endless, I ask you, Lord, to finish every good thing that you've begun in me! Psalm 138:6-8 TPT

Thanksgiving came around and I couldn't bring myself to cook so we went to my sister's house. My daughter was happy-go-lucky, and I couldn't figure out why. My world was falling apart, and she was running around laughing and playing. I got angry with her. She was writing in her diary when I snatched it from her, "you can't read that, that's my personal business" she said. "GIRL!!! You don't have any personal business!" I said very angrily. I'd had a few shots of vodka and was smoking weed with my sister's neighbor...back to self medicating, trying to numb myself.

I read the diary, looking for an admission of guilt, anything to say she was lying, but there was nothing and that made me angry. I prayed for God to reveal the truth. My husband said he was praying with m.e, telling me how heartbroken he was because he had to spend Thanksgiving away from us. I was so angry I started yelling at my daughter calling her a liar, asking her why, why was she lying. My sister started praying while I was yelling, and although her prayer was in another tongue, it was God Himself who allowed me to understand. I understood what came out of her mouth: He did it. She's not lying. Everything she said he did, he did. I heard it clear. It was so matter-of-fact. This was my answer. I called him and told him what I'd heard and he laughed at me. "You trying to say God told you that. "He wouldn't tell you something that's not true," he said. "Think about what you're saying. Listen to yourself. Why would God tell you something like that?" he asked. So I doubted what I'd heard. I felt so bad for accusing him of something like that. I apologized. "I know you want to believe her because your mother didn't believe you, but this is me, you know me. I'm your husband." he said. He was right, I thought. What's going on with me? What's wrong with me? I was unraveling. Fast.

February 1st. Our daughter's birthday. She asked if he could spend her birthday with us. I thought why not? CPS said he can be in the house as long as I'm here. I asked my oldest daughter if she'd mind him coming over, she said no, she didn't. I asked him if he wanted to come over and of course he did. He was so happy to come home and spend some time with us. He had been asking to come home, but something deep inside of me wasn't comfortable anymore. I couldn't say yes. I couldn't shake the fact that she accused him of such a thing. I did say he could come spend a few days, but when he was there I wasn't fully at ease like I'd been before everything happened. It was Saturday and Tamar was meeting that morning. Tamar, a ministry I'm in at church. It ministers to women and teen girls who have survived sexual abuse, rape, any type of unwanted sexual trauma...and I had survived it all by the grace of God. It was my third or fourth time there and I would've never been attending Tamar had it not been for the diligence of one of my QE sisters. I felt I had already dealt with my childhood sexual abuse and didn't need a class like Tamar. I said I wasn't going to attend that day because he was home, I wanted to soak up every minute with him since he'd been gone since November. Right when I'd decided not to go, I heard a voice say...go, and I was instructed to take my two oldest daughters with me, so we went. I couldn't fully focus in class because I knew he was home; I thought I should've stayed home. Just then, a woman came and sat next to me, seemingly talking to herself. "I hear you Holy Spirit. Yes Father, I hear you" she said.

My daughters sat away from me in the class, and when it was time to break out and go to our individual classes, they left. The woman said, "I feel so bad, that little girl's spirit is so grieved."

"What little girl?" I asked.

"The little girl with the blue coat on," she said. She was talking about my daughter. I didn't know what to say, I couldn't speak. Why is she saying my daughter's spirit is grieving?

After the knot left out my throat, I asked her what she meant. She took my hands and said "baby, she's not lying about what she told you."

How did she know what my daughter had told me? "Can you stay after class so we can pray with you and your children?" she asked. "Of course," I said. God had my full attention, this was the second time I was hearing...she's not lying. When class was over, myself and my daughters were put in the middle of a circle surrounded by five women. I was instructed to take off my shoes and coat and they began to pray. They prayed prayers that were heard in heaven, the Spirit of God moved in that room and totally consumed me. All the worry, doubt, fear, weight, and anxiety lifted off me. The women each took turns praying and prayed that heaviness, doubt and fear up off of me, the spirit of confusion and uncertainty. I thought I'd been praying for the truth to be revealed, but I was really praying that my daughter was lying; I could accept that she was lying rather than what she'd said...that he tried to have sex with her. My baby. He knew what I had lived through. He knew what it had done to me. As they prayed for me, in a vision I saw him, in bed with my daughter. I saw it. I had heard it when my sister prayed back in November, but this time, I couldn't deny it. I. Saw. It. When they were done praying, they told me to go home and walk in my house with my God given authority, and everything in my house that did not belong had to leave. They didn't know he was there. I hadn't told anyone, I guess I was fearful of judgment. After our prayer sessionended, I felt lighter, it felt like tons of bricks had been lifted off me. That afternoon I walked in my house with authority, like they told me. He was in the kitchen at the sink doing dishes and I said to him "God told me what you did and I didn't listen to Him because it was too hard for me to accept, but today he showed me. Now you tell me what you did." He started to cry, he could barely face me, he kept saying he was sorry... Sorry. Sorry, it kept repeating in my head. I was numb. I was in shock. I had to be in shock. I was amazingly calm. Unbelievably calm. The way I thought I would react, I didn't. My mind was saying kill him, but I couldn't move. I was numb. God's presence and overwhelming peace had fallen on me and I couldn't be anything but calm. Still.

You will keep him in perfect peace, whose mind is stayed on You, Because he trusts in You. Trust in the Lord forever, For in YAH, the Lord is everlasting strength. Isaiah 26:3-4 NKJV

You will keep the mind that is dependent on you in perfect peace, for it is trusting in you. Trust in the Lord forever, because in the Lord, the Lord himself is an everlasting rock! Isaiah 26:3-4 CSB

"Get your stuff and let's go." He couldn't even make eye contact with me and I was staring him down. He got his things and I dropped him off at BWI and took the seemingly extra long drive back home. Jesus! Jesus! Jesus! I couldn't believe it. I had the truth. After months of his lies and manipulation. My God, what had I done to my daughter? How could I not have believed her? Could she, would she forgive me? Suddenly I thought of my mom. I wept. It was me, in her shoes, all the years I wondered how...how do you not believe me, your child? What type of mother doesn't believe her child when she says this is what happened? It was me. I didn't believe my daughter. God was showing me what my mom felt. What she had went through. As hard as it was for me to believe my husband would do something like that to my child. It was just as hard for my mom to believe the man she loved would hurt me that way. I, as did she, believed we knew the men we loved so well. We trusted them. It was the rebellious pre-teen going through all these different changes that I didn't know. How wrong was I? I was literally walking in my mom's shoes. Looking in the mirror, I saw my mom. My heart broke for both of us. I cried and screamed to heaven, "I'M SORRY MOM! I'M SORRY!! I FORGIVE YOU!! I LOVE YOU MA!!!" Forgiveness for my mom had finally found its way to my heart. I also forgave my dad. I had resented him for not being a father to me. For everything I thought he'd done wrong, leaving me to fend for myself, choosing to love drugs more than me. It was this season in my life where I had to have some serious heart-to-heart conversations with God, and He asked me if I loved drugs more than my children, or was I bound by strongholds, memories of abuse and trauma like my dad had been. It didn't make him love me any less, like I didn't love my children any less. I was bound. Tormented by trauma, just like my dad...and my mom. Oh but Jesus came to set me free and reminded me that there is no condemnation in Him (*Romans 8:1*). My husband spent the next two months apologizing and asking if he could come back home, if he could have another chance. Every time I spoke with him, I could hear the Holy Spirit telling me to be still. Not to answer. Still. Be Still.

He had lied repeatedly to everyone about what happened. I told him if he was truly sorry, he needed to tell the truth. He wanted to come to church and get counseling. I felt like he needed to do whatever he needed or wanted to do on his own. I was angry, I was beyond angry. I wasn't going to pick him up for counseling and drop him off. Running back and forth to Baltimore. No!!! I cried so many tears. He was pleading with me to tell him our marriage could be saved, but I couldn't. He said he would tell his mom the truth, for me to just give him some time. He eventually did, and after all of her harsh words that she'd spoken about my daughter and I, she was silent. I asked him to tell the police the truth. When first questioned, he said my daughter was lying on him. I wanted him to tell the truth. He said if I'd go with him to the police station, he would. My daughter, he, and myself went to the police station and he confessed to having asked my daughter to have sex with him. He was arrested and held for 30 days. Even in all of this, I couldn't totally abandon him. I felt sorry for him, but I was so angry and disgusted with him. I was praying to God for guidance. I didn't know what to do. The Holy Spirit kept saying "be still." I tried to imagine what made him do it. Was it him going to prison at seventeen? Had he been abused in those fifteen years he'd served? I didn't know. As angry as I was with him, my heart broke for him and for my daughter.

I put money in his account so he could call. On a call one day, he asked if we could work things out. While he was talking to me, so was the Holy Spirit. The Holy Spirit told me I was in the way and that I needed to move. I told my husband I couldn't make that decision until I'd heard from God. Until God told me to, I wouldn't do anything. He got upset, told me to have a nice life, and hung up the phone. WHAT!!!!?? I felt a cussing spirit rise up inside of me. After I accepted that call he hung up on me. I thought, Ok. It's all good. Well, it was far from good, but ok. About three weeks passed, and he called. He was due in court April 18, 2016. I went to court, and found out that the State's Attorney changed his bail from "No Bail" to a fifteen-thousand dollar bail. When I got home, another inmate's mother called me. She told me my husband asked her to call me and give me the name of a bail bondsman so I could post his bail! IS HE FREAKING CRAZY?!!? I'm not paying his bail!! "Tell him I'll call his mom," I told her.

His mom informed me she wasn't paying it either. "He had made this bed, threw his family away, and he would have to go through this on his own, with no crutches" she said." For fifteen years in prison and ten years in his marriage I have been his crutch, but not this time" she said. His mom felt like she'd done the fifteen years with him, now he was on his own. For me, I had a tough time pulling away, but I relied on God for strength. Then something happened...GRACE! God gave him grace.

He was released on April 19th with all charges dropped. Sexual assault of a minor and Second Degree Child Abuse (because of the spanking), all dropped. Because he didn't touch her private area, or make her touch his, (so they thought) they couldn't charge him with sexual assault and because he was her step-dad, they didn't charge him with assault for the spanking. They called it "grooming", preparing her to have sex with him, and there was no charge for that, no law existed about grooming at the time. He was released, free and clear, with no sex offender registration or anything. I sat my daughter down to explain that he was being released. She was upset. She wanted to know why he was getting away with it. I couldn't explain it to her. I didn't understand it myself. He called and asked if I would pick him up from the jail. I said I would, but after I thought about it, I was furious. "I'm not going to get him, he needs to call his aunt to come down here from Baltimore to pick him up." I said. My daughter looked at me and said "go get him mom, It's ok. I forgive him." I was so shocked. I couldn't believe it. She said she forgave him and I knew in my heart I didn't. I went to get him from jail. The ride was extra long and mostly silent, besides him asking me to let him come home that night. I was full of so much emotion, I could only shake my head no. He asked me to please think about it. He told me God had changed him while he was locked up. He said God took away the taste of alcohol and drugs and he was ready to be the man God was calling him to be. On and off for years he used heroin. I had given him an ultimatum about two years ago and told him it was the drugs or us. He promised he was done with it. It was the first time in ten years he said the words out of his mouth "I know I have a problem with heroin and I'm going to get help. I'll show you" he said. His words fell on deaf ears.

Be still, and know that I am God; I will be exalted among the nations, I will be exalted in the earth! Psalm 46:10 NKJV

"Stop your fighting, and know that I am God, exalted among the nations, exalted

on the earth."

Psalm 46:10 CSB

Surrender your anxiety. Be still and realize that I am God. I am God above all the nations. And I am exalted throughout the whole earth. Psalm 46:10 TPT

I dropped him off at BWI. He told me all the things I ever wanted to hear, things I waited years to hear. How God had finally broken him down in jail, and he was going to prove to me that he was the man God had for me and our children. He said God showed him he was going to die if he didn't stop. He literally said "God showed me my death." I don't want to die and leave a bad taste in nobody's mouth. I want my family back. Whatever I gotta do to get my family back, I'll do it, he said. On April 20th, the next morning, we talked via video chat. He said he was going to see about a job and he would call me when he got back in the house. In that instant, my phone died, and he was gone. I later went to class at church, All Things New, a class for people who struggle with unwanted same-sex attraction. It was about 6:20 pm. I almost stepped out in the hallway to call him because he never called back, but I thought, no, he's either going to be a man of his word, or not, so I didn't call him. That morning at about 1:30 am I got a call from his mom, "open the door, we're outside" she said. I looked out the window, and her car was in my driveway. I thought he'd asked his mom to drive all the way here from Baltimore to ask me to let him come home. I opened the door to his mom, stepdad, aunt, her male friend, and her son. They came in, I was waiting for him to come in. His mom asked me to sit down. I'd never seen the look on her face or in her eyes before. It was sorrowful. It spoke to me. "I don't want to sit down, where is he?"

I asked. "Please sit down," she said. No! I don't want to sit down, I shouted.

"He's gone," she said. Gone where? Gone? What!? She fell on the couch crying, "he's dead!!" she screamed. I bolted out the front door running down the long rocky, glass, and gravel road screaming his name. "I'm here! I'm here!" I shouted! PLEASE!!! I'M HERE!!! PLEASE!! PLEASE!!! I'M HERE!!! I was in a daze. I have to get to him. I can speak life into him. I NEED TO GET TO HIM!!! PLEASE!! PLEASE!! NO!! NO!! NO!!! But he was gone. Gone. Gone. GONE!! GONE??? My mind started to think..."What did I do wrong!!?" I turned my back on him. I left him alone, why had I not agreed to counseling? Why had I not let him come home? Then I remembered, nothing can happen without God's approval and that made me angry.

They said he was walking to his aunt's house and collapsed in her front yard. He would lay there for almost an hour before anyone came to help him. Someone called 911, they tried to revive him but couldn't. I got a call in the morning from the medical examiner asking me questions about his health and if he used drugs. I told her his history and she said after they examined his body they would call and give me the cause of death. She said if they had to do a toxicology test, that meant drugs were involved. She called back the next day and said the toxicology tests were needed. They couldn't find the cause of death after examination of his organs. I got a call in about a week or so that confirmed what I'd already known. When I got the call from the medical examiner, he asked if I wanted to sit down before he gave me the results. "I'm driving," I said, you can tell me." Morphine Intoxication. Good luck to you ma'am" he said. For years, we had struggled in our marriage because of his drug use. He'd stop for a while, or maybe not. Maybe he just learned how to hide it from me. Maybe I didn't want to see it because it would force me to make him choose and

I didn't think he would choose us. Maybe I believed him when he said no one is gonna want you with 8 kids. Maybe I believed I deserved it, the abuse. The presence of God came and dwelled with me during the preparation for and during his funeral, it was God's Spirit and I alone. God knew that was the only way I could be present there, to be with Him, in His presence. His glory filled me and it felt like angels were dancing around me, comforting me, praying over me, interceding on my behalf. They led me to a place of total worship and adoration for Christ Jesus and His mercy on my children and I.

Blessed be the God and Father of our Lord Jesus Christ, the Father of mercies and God of all comfort, who comforts us in all our tribulation, that we may be able to comfort those who are in any trouble, with the comfort with which we ourselves are comforted by God. For as the sufferings of Christ abound in us, so our consolation also abounds through Christ.

2 Corinthians 1:3-5 NKJV

Blessed be the God and Father of our Lord Jesus Christ, the Father of mercies and the God of all comfort. He comforts us in all our affliction, so that we may be able to comfort those who are in any kind of affliction, through the comfort we ourselves receive from God. For just as the sufferings of Christ overflow to us, so also through Christ our comfort overflows.

2 Corinthians 1:3-5 CSB

All praises belong to the God and Father of our Lord Jesus Christ. For he is the Father of tender mercy and the God of endless comfort. He always comes alongside to comfort us in every suffering so that we can come alongside those who are in any painful trial. We can bring them this same comfort that God has poured out upon us. And just as we experience the abundance of Christ's own sufferings, even more of God's comfort will cascade upon us through our union with Christ.

2 Corinthians 1:3-5 TPT

What the Redeemer Has Given Me: Purpose

God is with me and my eight children that He blessed me with. My oldest is my strong, beautiful, courageous, talented, outspoken, and very lit daughter. My second oldest, my beautiful, talented, funny, hardworking, and loving daughter. My third oldest, my handsome son who is very intellectual, kind, smart, generous, and caring. Fourth is my beautiful daughter, who is very artistic, smart, creative, and was accepted into a Talented and Gifted school. She is also a chef and baker. Fifth is my daughter who is a beautiful, fearless, brave, talented, basketball player, who also loves to bake and sing. Sixth is my beautiful, sensitive, talented, and very loving daughter who also loves to sing. Seventh, my bonus daughter that I took custody of when her mom, my first cousin, died from cancer. She's also very beautiful, loving, caring, and happy-go-lucky, in spite of all she has endured in her short lifetime. Before she came to me, she had lived with her grandad, my uncle, after his daughter, her mom, died. The house they lived in caught on fire, and everyone made it out except my eleven year old cousin, she died In that fire. My last and youngest daughter, she's beautiful, full of love and energy, and a gymnast. While having a conversation with my sixth daughter one day, (she had issues sometimes using the bathroom), I was telling her I was going to put some olive oil on her bottom to help comfort her, my bonus daughter said "that's what dad used to do to me" he would rub oil on my butt. My mind was still processing the words That's. What. Dad. Used. To. Do. To. Me. My son started yelling "you're lying!!" "Stop lying!!" I calmed my son down and took her upstairs to speak with her in private. I asked her to tell me what dad used to do. She told me he would tell her she hadn't cleaned herself good so he had to clean her with baby wipes and put his fingers in her bottom. I asked her why she didn't tell me, she said he told her she couldn't tell me or the other kids. She said he would make the other kids go outside to play. She couldn't tell anyone. He told her he had to do that because she wasn't cleaning herself well. She didn't realize what he'd done was wrong. I let her go back downstairs and I went into my prayer closet and collapsed. Wailing. A sound was coming out of me that sounded like a wounded animal, something unrecognizable. When I looked up, My oldest daughter was standing over me. "Are you ok mom? Do you believe her?" She asked. It took me a minute to speak, but I said "yes, I believe her, why would she say something like that, she's six". My daughter gave me a look, took a deep breath and said "he did the same thing to me" she let out a long deep exhale...that same long intentional exhale I let out after revealing my own sexual abuse when I was her same age. Twelve. I fell back to the floor, in my prayer closet. Weeping and wailing. What is this God!!? WHAT IS THIS!!!? PLEASE!! I CAN'T TAKE ANYMORE!!! PLEASE!!! HELP ME!!! IF YOU DON'T HELP ME, I'M NOT GOING TO MAKE IT!!! I had never cried releasing the sounds that were coming from me, it didn't sound human. I called one of my sisters from the Tamar Ministry, she prayed me up off the floor. I had been in the process of looking for a new house because we needed a new start. When he died, I could no longer be in my house alone. One of the Reverends at my church let me use her office, so after I put my children on the school bus everyday I would go to my church, in her office to cry and pray until my children got out of school, I did this every day for months. My ministry sister said God had to let all secrets be exposed so I could leave it all there, in that house. Not take any secrets with me to our new house. JESUS!! Oh the grace that found me!! Through the unimaginable, God graced me to stand! He taught me how to rely on Him and use His strength. He drew me nearer to Him. He showed me His strength was made perfect in my weakness! He taught me how to commune with Him, to abide with Him! He taught me to see myself the way He sees me! He showed me my father's love for me! He showed me my mother's love for me! He removed the veil that had covered my eyes! He unclogged my ears to hear Him clearly! I am who He says I am! A survivor! An overcomer! A daughter of a King! Through Him, I have been restored! He showed His love for me. Through my memories He allowed me to look back and recognize He was with me all along! He showed me my worth, and reminded me that He has never made anything or anyone that doesn't have value in His eyes! Even my husband. He told me he belonged to Him! I was able to forgive my husband, truly forgive him. That didn't mean I wasn't still hurt, but God is a God who restores. He has given me beauty for ashes. I play my tape back and I'm in awe of God, how he favored my children by favoring me. He continues to impress me, to inspire me, to captivate me, to draw me nearer.

I am so blessed, and felt God's presence more than ever before. I didn't think I would make it through some days, but He held me up and gave me strength each day. Every second of every day.

I was done with being in a backslidden state. I totally surrendered my life to Jesus and became so hungry for Him, I sought Him like never before. He was there waiting for me, and welcomed me with arms stretched wide. Through it all, I walked into my purpose. I was given an opportunity to attend to a conference with MCASA: The Maryland Coalition Against Sexual Assault. They had come to my church to have a seminar on safe touching. Recognizing the red flags dealing with sexual abuse. That would be the beginning of my journey to become an advocate for people who've survived sexual abuse. I've been blessed to hear and answer the call, and to finally be in obedience with God and His will for my life. I've learned the effects of trauma and how it manifests when untreated. I now volunteer at University of

Maryland DV/SAC Domestic Violence Sexual Assault Center, I am a member of HTTF PG County, Human Trafficking Task Force Prince Georges County, I am a member of SART, Sexual Assault Response Team Prince Georges County, and Founder and COO of Marilyn Lacy Ministries, a 501(c)(3) faith-based organization helping survivors of sexual abuse. It's helping me to see myself and others differently. I realize now the trauma my mom and her siblings lived through. My dad and his siblings also. I need people to know we have to be accountable for getting the help we need to heal. Matthew 19:26 tells us: 'with God all things are possible" Luke 1:37 reads "For Nothing is impossible with God". I never imagined I'd be able to smile and worship in the church where I stood in front of the caskets of my mother and my husband two years apart. I remember walking out of my husband's funeral, hand on his casket saying, "God whatever needs to go, let it go with him, please don't let anything remain God". I had told myself I would never step foot back in that sanctuary again. That's what grace does. It allows you to do what you think is impossible.

My Pastor, John K. Jenkins Sr. said, "Whatever has burdened your heart, that is your purpose." I've been burdened for years to help those who have been or are being abused. I didn't know the beast would show its ugly head in my house, with my own children. God was and is ever present. What the enemy meant for evil, God made it good. I would have never imagined I or my children would have to endure such heartache and pain. The heartbreaking task of caring for my mom, I didn't know why I had to watch my mom die. In my alone time with God, He asked, "did you watch her die or did you watch her live and fight...don't you see the grace I gave to you?" He changed my perspective and I realized I'd watched her live. I watched her fight. For seven years she fought. I remembered that night in the hospital she was yelling... fight! Fight! Fight! God let me hear her screaming those words so when

I felt like giving up, I'd remember her words, Fight! Fight! Fight! God knew He had equipped me to handle everything that I would have to face, even if I didn't feel like it at the time. He knew if He had taken her any sooner, I wouldn't have made it. Everything God allows is to build us, not to break us. He put into perspective my thought that was once...why did I have to go through so much...He let me see there was never a time in my life where I was anywhere He was not. Through it all, childhood sex abuse, rape, drug dealing and drug use, prostitution, attempted murder by a boyfriend, domestic violence etc...God's hand remained over me. He continues to strengthen me and build my character and He has given me ministry through all of it. All of it!

I've learned to love the person I see in the mirror, and I look forward to what God has for my children and I. He has never failed, He is Faithful. He wants a relationship with us. Though He has surrounded me (us) with people (my village) that were and are willing to help me (us) and pray for me, He wanted me, needed me in a place where I would recognize Him as my source, and pray for myself. Learn to speak His word over my children, family, friends and myself. The Word of God is easily accessible to us. I had to stop relying on myself and others to do for me what I desperately needed God to do, what only He could do through my relationship with Jesus Christ. He has redeemed me and will do the same for you. He loves us so much. He's such a gentleman; He won't force Himself on you. You have to invite Him into your heart. First, we must believe He is who the Bible says He is: The true and living Son of God. He died for our sins, was buried, and rose on the third day. He lives! He got up with all-power in His hand. Glory Hallelujah!! Understand we must become prayer warriors not afraid of war! There is no warrior without war. HE HAS WELL EQUIPPED US! Stop fighting in the flesh! This is a spiritual war! We must see, hear and pray in the Spirit.

I found that some people want God to be their Savior, but they don't want Him to be their Lord. It's necessary that we surrender every area of our lives to Him. We have to give up our will for His! We must allow Him full control! It's a must that He's our LORD and SAVIOR. We cannot have one without the other. At my last visit with my cardiologist he said my heart is functioning at sixty-five percent with no signs I ever had Congestive Heart Failure. I've not been admitted to the hospital since November 2015. I know God as Healer, Restorer, Deliverer, Mind Regulator... He's done more than I could ask or think.

If you want to accept Christ into your life, please pray this prayer: ***Dear Lord, I acknowledge that I am a sinner. I believe Jesus Christ is Your Son and that He died on the cross for my sins, was buried and rose from the dead. I repent of my sins and turn toward Jesus. I invite Him into my heart and into my life to rule and reign. I thank You dear Lord for saving me. In Jesus' name. Amen.***

If you sincerely prayed that prayer, you are now in the family of God! I am excited for what God is going to do in your life, because of your faith! I would love to hear from you, please feel free to bless me with your testimonies.

Therefore, if anyone is in Christ, he is a new creation; old things have passed away; behold, all things have become new.
2 Corinthians 5:17 NKJV

Therefore, if anyone is in Christ, he is a new creation; the old has passed away, and see, the new has come! 2 Corinthians 5:17 CSB

Now, if anyone is enfolded into Christ, he has become an entirely new person. All that is related to the order has vanished. Behold, everything is fresh and new. 2 Corinthians 5:17 TPT

Then He who sat on the throne said, "Behold, I make all things new." And He said to me, "Write, for these words are true and faithful." Revelation 21:5 NKJV

Then the one seated on the throne said, "Look, I am making everything new." He also said, "write, because these words are faithful and true." Revelation 21:5 CSB

And God-Enthroned spoke to me and said, "Consider this! I am making everything to be new and fresh. Write down at once all that I have told you, because each word is trustworthy and dependable." Revelation 21:5 TPT

In His service, Marilyn Lacy

Facebook: Marilyn Lacy Marilyn Lacy Ministries
Instagram: Marilyn L Lacy
Periscope: @iammarilynlacy
Twitter: @marilyn_lacy
mlacyministries@gmail.com

www.ingramcontent.com/pod-product-compliance
Lightning Source LLC
Chambersburg PA
CBHW031428290426
44110CB00011B/567